THE BEST FOR BABIES
Expert Advice for Assessing Infant-Toddler Programs

Alice Sterling Honig, PhD

Bulk Purchase

Gryphon House books are available for special premiums and sales promotions as well as for fund-raising use. Special editions or book excerpts also can be created to specifications. For details, contact the Director of Marketing at Gryphon House.

Disclaimer

Gryphon House, Inc., cannot be held responsible for damage, mishap, or injury incurred during the use of or because of activities in this book. Appropriate and reasonable caution and adult supervision of children involved in activities and corresponding to the age and capability of each child involved are recommended at all times. Do not leave children unattended at any time. Observe safety and caution at all times.

The BEST for Babies

for Babies

Expert Advice
for Assessing
Infant-Toddler Programs

from **Dr. Alice Honig**

Gryphon House, Inc.
Lewisville, NC

Copyright

©2014 Alice Sterling Honig

Published by Gryphon House, Inc.
P. O. Box 10, Lewisville, NC 27023
800.638.0928; 877.638.7576 (fax)
Visit us on the web at www.gryphonhouse.com.

Cover photograph courtesy of Shutterstock.com © 2014.

Library of Congress Cataloging-in-Publication Data
Honig, Alice S.
 The best for babies : expert advice for assessing infant-toddler programs / Dr. Alice Sterling Honig.
     pages cm
 Includes bibliographical references and index.
 ISBN 978-0-87659-554-1
 1. Child care--United States. 2. Child development--United States. 3. Education, Preschool--United States. 4. Education, Preschool--Activity programs--United States. I. Title.
 HQ778.63.H66 2014
 362.70973--dc23
                          2014009466

Table of Contents

Acknowledgments

I would like to acknowledge with grateful appreciation all the loving care of perceptive and skilled caregivers and parents who have cherished little children over the years, whose interactions with the children have illuminated theoretical and research findings about developmentally appropriate practices in harmonious and vivid ways.

I thank with deep appreciation Editor-in-Chief Diane Ohanesian and the Gryphon House staff for their dedication and gracious support in making this book available for caregivers, parents, and directors.

I thank my children, Larry, Madeleine, and Jonathan, for the privilege of helping me learn through years of practice, through mistakes, and through positive interactions how to nourish each of them through the years and help them grow into the deeply committed and admirable parents they have been to my grown grandchildren.

PREFACE

Awareness of the importance of early education for children continues to grow not only among developed nations but also across the world. Quality early childhood education (ECE) is recognized increasingly as a pathway to help children grow out of lives of poverty, a route toward school success, and a helpful support for children on the journey toward later satisfaction in their professional and personal lives.

Tools for assessing quality programs mostly have been based on assessing outcomes for young children, such as knowledge of ABCs or overall readiness for kindergarten. Assessments may encompass a wide variety of programmatic aspects, including level of teacher education, cultural norms for child classroom behaviors, degree of child autonomy and choice of activity allowed, culturally accepted discipline techniques, and child-teacher ratios. Some assessments include ratings of the availability of printed program curricula; abundance of materials; toys and equipment; classroom ambience, such as lighting, wall coverings, and carpets; spatial arrangements; child gender ratios in the classroom; length of daily schedules; richness of teacher talk with children; and relationship of staff with families.

Many tools for assessing early childhood classrooms focus on structural variables; they predominantly emphasize child outcomes. And, indeed, research has shown the importance of some of the variables listed. For example, research on child-teacher ratios has revealed the vulnerability—as shown by their distressed behaviors—of male (but not female) children in group settings when there are more children per preschool teacher (Bornstein et al., 2006).

Other research has revealed that a teacher who holds a four-year college degree in early childhood education is more likely to be identified among teachers who are rated as "less authoritarian in their childrearing attitudes than caregivers with no training" (Arnett, 1989). Teacher training has been undertaken to enrich language with children and thus enhance quality of child experiences in care. Teachers with training in how to extend and lengthen conversational exchanges with young children were observed immediately after training (although not several months later) to extend their conversations with children (Honig and Martin, 2009). Significantly, teacher preparation, skills, and empathy have been shown to be the primary factors in children's positive outcomes after their preschool experiences. When such teacher skills are lacking, then poorer outcomes for children have been found. Caribbean researchers concluded that "rural Guyanese children in classrooms with teachers who had high school qualifications did not seem prepared for primary school" (Roopnarine, 2013).

A study of nearly three thousand children in 703 state-funded preschool classrooms in nine U.S. states concluded that two factors in particular proved to be the best predictors of child outcomes: The quality of teacher-child interactions consistently proved to be the strongest predictor of children's learning, followed by the learning environment (Sabol et al., 2013). From a content analysis of more than seventy-six studies, La Paro et al. (2012) also emphasized that the depth of quality must be factored in when assessing classroom quality.

Difficulties may arise in trying to characterize center quality by overall quality-rating scales across classrooms. Such ratings may miss the essential differences in interaction quality among teachers with the children they serve—even among those teachers serving the same age groups in a facility. Capturing center-level quality based on average environmental rating scale scores could then fail to identify within-center quality differences in different classrooms. Identifying these in-classroom differences is necessary, for example, as directors and educational personnel in resource and referral agencies are planning programs to provide training for those teachers needing further enhancement of their knowledge and skills. Such identification could even be useful in identifying "master teachers" in a facility who could mentor new teachers or those needing wider practice in using positive styles and skills with young children or a deeper understanding of child development.

Given the critical importance of caregiver-child interactions in promoting cognitive, language, and social-emotional learning in young children, the care quality checklist items in this book focus strongly on the kind, quality, intensiveness, and extensiveness of the behaviors and interactions between a teacher or care provider and each child. The checklist provides a way to assess each interpersonal relationship—its quality in enhancing the learning and living experiences for young children. As a result, directors and teachers can consider the ratings as they identify ways to optimize the outcomes for each child.

Each of the checklist items has explanatory descriptive materials that can help each teacher focus even deeper on how to craft, creatively modify, and extend her interactions to meet the needs of each precious small person in her care. Examples and illustrative anecdotes clarify items to ensure that trainers and directors will find the checklist useful. The care quality checklist can be used to help teachers flourish and feel deepening pride in their professional expertise and careers as they continue to guide children's learning and well-being.

THE IMPORTANCE OF QUALITY CHILD CARE

Loving, knowledgeable, and skilled caregivers provide the priceless ingredients for raising emotionally healthy children who will be enthusiastic learners and work hard to achieve their unique life goals. Given this kind of start in life, children are likely to grow into caring, concerned citizens who will, in turn, contribute to helping others grow up to become productive, creative, kind human beings. High-quality early care programs that emphasize regular staff training have been shown to yield impressive societal benefits:

- lower percentages of school-age children who needed to repeat classes;
- increased self-control;
- lower adolescent delinquency rates;
- less delinquency recidivism;
- more total years of education, including more college education; and
- more months per year as adult taxpaying workers.

In times of financial hardship, child care centers may face budget cuts that decrease the possibility of funds for extensive staff training or staff monitoring. George Morrison (2012), professor of early education and author of "Racing to the Bottom," has grimly noted, "some preschool programs, faced with increasing numbers of underemployed and out-of-work parents, cut their tuition, desperately trying to make their programs more affordable for the new generation of parents and families. These policies, of course, just accelerate the free fall into poor-quality programs."

Research findings on the positive effects of quality care are beginning to percolate through other parts of society beyond child care and educational constituencies and some state governments. The greater the involvement of many different constituencies among citizens who become aware of the benefits of quality early care, the more likely that legal and financial as well as professional educational supports for quality care can become available through legislative focus and action.

Defining Quality Care

How is quality in early childhood education and child care defined? Many of the key elements for providing excellent nurturing care and learning opportunities for young children have been confirmed in research and clinical studies:

- Encouraging positive peer interactions in dramatic play
- Expressive daily book reading
- Galvanizing group projects
- Rich oral-language interactions
- Specific use of open-ended questions to promote thinking skills

- Strategies to improve numerical understandings
- Personal reflectivity
- Encouraging mindfulness and self-regulation
- Cognitive flexibility and sustained attention to tasks
- Fostering friendships
- Secure attachment
- Home-visitation techniques to enhance family involvement and to build secure infant-parent attachment

Additionally, teachers need further skills and specific techniques for nurturing and working with children who have special needs or who have experienced early abuse or trauma.

Numerous rating scales and assessment instruments are available for monitoring child achievement and progress in a wide range of developmental areas. Many of these scales, checklists, and rating instruments are particularly useful to monitor child attainments in child care settings. However, instruments for assessing the quality of provider care and for assessing the effectiveness of caregiver training efforts are in far shorter supply.

The need for quality rating and improvement systems (QRIS) is becoming recognized at federal levels. Recently, the Center for American Progress released a report titled *Increasing the Effectiveness and Efficiency of Existing Public Investments in Early Childhood Education*, which includes recommendations for the federal government to enhance the quality of child care. The report urges partnering with states to build assessments and assessment systems that demonstrate that standards are being met. The report further recommends that the federal government should help determine the optimal set of skills and information that caregivers need to know, to boost the efficacy of preparation programs for early childhood program staff. The report emphasizes the importance of implementing a consistent, state-of-the-art approach to high-quality professional development.

Finding ways to assess the quality of caregiving for young children has been a challenge. The National Association for the Education of Young Children (NAEYC), Head Start, individual states, and numerous child-development research centers have developed tools for evaluating the environments and quality of care in child care centers.

Turnover, not only of staff but also of directors, is a worrisome factor in its impact on quality. De-Souza (2012) conducted in-depth interviews with center directors to find out how they perceive or implement continuity of care. The NAEYC supports programmatic efforts to ensure quality of care by keeping infants and toddlers together with the same teachers during their first three years in child care. Interviews revealed that most directors were vague as to the meaning of this marker of quality care for infants and toddlers. Most directors explained that operationalizing continuity of care would be too daunting a task. The directors pointed out their many responsibilities, which include fulfilling age-specific teacher-child ratios, meeting payroll budget, arranging for care when a teacher calls in sick, and meeting teacher needs. Moreover, De-Souza found that almost half of those hardworking directors, interviewed in depth, had quit their jobs within a year after the interviews and could no longer even be reached.

Staff and director turnover rates need to be taken into account in determining when to assess quality of care. When there is turmoil from turnover, it may be advisable to wait a few months until staff stability is in place before using any tool to assess quality of child care.

Teacher-Child Intimate Interactions

In a safe environment, highly skilled and well-trained caregivers are the most important ingredients of quality child care. Fancy furniture, stenciled wall-decoration patterns, and expensive toys do not define quality care. Tender, tuned-in, creative, and genuinely cherishing persons help children deepen their trust in adults. Trust is a four-way system: Adults have to trust their feelings of kindness, their bountiful reserves of patience, and their deep delight in each unique child in their care. Adults have to trust each child's signals of distress and try promptly to interpret those signals and meet that child's needs for nurturance. When children deeply trust that they are loved and lovable—that they are totally accepted despite garbled speech, juice spills, toileting accidents, and loud wails when upset—then they trust themselves to try even when they encounter frustrations. These children are able to devote all their life energies to growing into capable, hardworking, and joyous persons. They can concentrate on learning language, new skills, how to navigate environments, how to work toys, and how to feel comfortable with reasonable social rules. These children can, in turn, learn to reach out with empathy and caring toward others because, from their earliest days, they have experienced empathy and kind, intimate interactions.

Without kind, intimate interactions, little persons may grow up carrying a core in their beings that remains anxious or belligerent for years. A teenage mother with two little ones once assured me that both of her children were "bad, really bad." How sad for little ones to grow up feeling that conviction about themselves from the beginning of their lives! Without trust and intimacy, children feel tense from the earliest years—despite their defiant swaggers, blustering and aggressive behaviors, and indifference to adult entreaties or rules. Not having felt rock-solid in their innermost beings that they are precious, unique, important people, they may misinterpret others' feelings. They may expect others to be mean and uncaring, because they never feel truly acknowledged and understood by an attentive, caring adult.

When a child is held, given leisurely time to play, offered safe and interesting materials to explore, and experiences intimate, one-on-one interactions with a special adult, she will grow and flourish. Secure that she is cherished and safe, the child can devote all her energies to learning. The child will delight in and safely explore the world, gain receptive and expressive language skills, and forge those habits of attentiveness and persistence that make learning possible.

INGREDIENTS OF CARE QUALITY

The care quality checklist provided in this book defines quality specifically in terms of the relationships and interactions between the caregiver and each child in the provider's care in that facility. Thus, it is important initially to focus on what components of these personal interactions and relationships are essential for a caregiver to learn during professional preparation. In discussing caregiver interactions in this book, the terms *teacher*, *care provider*, and *caregiver* will be used interchangeably.

Understanding Developmental Milestones

Knowledge of developmental milestones is crucial. There are many online resources to help caregivers understand children's development. PBS offers a useful site called The ABCs of Child Development: Developmental Milestones for Your Child's First Five Years, available at http://www.pbs.org/wholechild/abc/index.html. First Years offers a helpful chart detailing the milestones in hearing, speech, language, and cognition in a child's first eight years of life. It is available at http://firstyears.org/miles/chart.pdf.

Use intimate interactions with little ones to learn about the unique needs and stages of each child's development, where each child is, and what he requires. For example, some toddlers may have lots of single words but may not put two words together until they are nearly two years old. Once, while I was diapering one child, I heard another child scream. I called out, "No hitting, Luanne. That hurts." She answered back tartly and clearly: "I did not hit her; I bit her!" Her language skills were in awesome supply, although her ability to treat others gently needed more guidance.

Babies and young children often reach developmental milestones at different times. Some babies understand lots of talk but struggle to coordinate tongue, palate, teeth, vocal cords, and other articulators to pronounce words clearly. Some toddlers can carry a tune so well that a parent may be surprised to hear a toddler humming a song a teacher has taught the children. An older toddler may no longer scribble but may draw the semblance of a kitty or a tree. Tune in to the gifts of each child. Tune in to the timetables of each child. One child may learn to use the potty early but have trouble with an easy puzzle. Another toddler may expertly navigate the room after his teacher has wiped his nose and asked him to put the tissue in a wastebasket. Spatial skills, language skills, reasoning skills, and social skills—all develop at different times for different children.

Narrow Windows and Wide Windows

Knowledge of developmental milestones can guide expectations and decisions about using special techniques and supports with children. Because of low wage scales in the field, many caregivers have not had the educational opportunities to become thoroughly familiar with early child-development milestones. Additionally, specialized training opportunities for caregivers may be locally in short supply or too expensive. However, knowing what to expect at each age and stage is important information for caregivers to have. Learning milestones for each arena of development helps a teacher know when to feel comfortable that all is well, when to wonder, and when to worry.

Some windows of development are narrow, and some are wider. A skill with a narrow window develops within a short period of time. Armed with information about what is normative within limits, child care providers have powerful tools for decision making. For example, hand development follows a timetable such that the tightly folded fist of the newborn opens to a curved palm by three to four months. Then, an infant will swat or bat at the interesting mobile that his teacher has hung over the crib. By six months, a baby can corral and rake in one-inch blocks on a tabletop using his whole hand.

An infant's ability to pick up a tiny object with just the thumb and forefinger (called *superior pincer prehension*) has a narrow window of development. Usually this learning is accomplished by eleven or twelve months of age. If a child has not demonstrated dexterity in picking up items with his thumb and forefinger by this time, a caregiver may decide that it is necessary to make extra efforts, using food morsels creatively, to help the child with that emerging skill. Or, a provider may decide that a fourteen-month-old baby's continued use of the whole hand rather than pincer prehension to rake in a Cheerio is truly a reason for worry, and the caregiver may decide to ask the center director to consider arranging a more formal assessment. The caregiver who knows that a particular baby was born two months prematurely will realize the need for patience. That baby may need more "catch-up" time to develop pincer-prehension dexterity.

Precise wrist control comes in much later and depends on full myelination of the great motor neurons that make fine controls possible for different motor abilities. The white, fatty sheath of myelin that clothes each nerve fiber and permits quick voluntary control of muscles, fine wrist control, or steady walking develops slowly. Wrist control can take as long as two years for some babies. Thus, teachers should expect that some toddlers will spill milk or have trouble trying to tip their sippy cups far enough to get milk into their mouths—frustrating for caregivers as well as for babies! The perceptive teacher is aware of how much skill wrist control requires and will support that development, such as through offering beanbag toss games.

Some skills have genetically based timetables. Walking and dentition (when teeth appear) each have a strong genetic component. One baby may be born with a tooth. Another may not get a first tooth until he is a year old; he will need to eat strained food longer because he cannot yet chew and might choke on the finger foods that the first baby relishes. Even chewing develops in stages. Up-and-down chewing motions are earliest. The ability to perform full rotary chewing is the most highly developed kind of chewing.

Locomotion development has a wide window. Some babies creep about easily on the floor by nine months of age. Others take longer to become mobile. Some babies walk upright before the age of one year. Others toddle with a wide-apart gait at nearly one and a half years. The teacher who is aware of locomotion development will provide sturdy furniture that a baby can pull up on and use to cruise along while holding on. Providing such important props supports baby's early attempts to navigate the world vertically.

Toilet learning has a very wide window for completion. Learning to use the potty consistently during the daytime may take place anywhere from eighteen months (more likely for some females) to three or four years, but the ability to stay dry during the night may take far longer for some children, particularly for males. Some children are unable to control night urination and may need diapers until kindergarten time. A child who has an older sibling may desire to sit on the potty and pee like her sibling does. A teacher can simply allow her to try and can place a stack of picture books on the floor for her to look at as she sits on the potty. Other children may not learn to use a potty consistently for years. One bright five-and-a-half-year-old, still in diapers, cheerfully assured his worried parents, "When we go to Grandpa's house for Thanksgiving, then I will use the potty." And he did!

Other skills require far more personal support and creative encouragement. Teacher ingenuity can be crucially important when a child is shy or inexperienced in the social skills required for playing harmoniously with other children. Older toddlers and most preschoolers engage zestfully in pretend play with peers. They play house and pretend to be family members or friends on a shopping trip. They play superheroes. Dressing in yellow rain slickers, preschoolers act as energetic firefighters bravely putting out a fire. Children happily use dress-up clothes as imaginary props in their play. A preschooler who lacks skills for pretend play will surely need insightful and creative teacher assistance to help him learn group-entry skills, ways to offer to engage in play with peers, and possible scenarios to use to engage with peers in pretend play.

I recall a toddler who wanted to play with some older children. Outside in the snow, two preschoolers were lugging snow in a wagon to use in creating a snowman together. They rejected little Orin's bid to play with them. Orin then offered, "I can help you pull the wagon full of snow." Orin's social skills were well honed, and he found a way to be accepted into the big kids' play!

Noticing the variability for each developmental advance for each child sharpens a caregiver's understanding of timetables and how different children reach milestones at different times. In addition, this understanding helps a caregiver exhibit deep patience and compassion for each child as he works toward mastery of each new ability. Thus, learning milestones for newly emerging behaviors involves not only knowing about when a given skill emerges but also understanding the normative *range* for development of that skill. This provides helpful information for decisions about when to wonder, when to worry, or when to galvanize additional consultations and supports.

Language Progress

Very early, infants produce throaty vowel sounds called *coos*. A caregiver who responds with genuine interest to these cooing sounds can carry on a "conversation" with a baby a few months old for as long as a dozen cooing turns. By six months, babies often combine easy consonants, such as *p, m, n, b,* and *d,* with a vowel to create *pa, ma, na, ba,* and *da.* When these sounds are doubled, they sound just like the early names for delighted family members: *papa, mama, nana, baba,* and *dada.*

By the end of the first year, babies start babbling nonreduplicated consonant-vowel combinations, often with earnest intonations, as if they are truly trying to communicate with a caregiver. An adult who responds happily to these early babbles often receives a torrent of babbles in response. Babies engage in vigorous turn-taking talk with vocally responsive caregivers. Infants at this age are often using a few eloquent single words such as *hi, bye, up,* and *more.* They enjoy making animal sounds, such as *woof-woof,* especially when seeing the family pet or looking at a book with colorful pictures of familiar animals.

Caregivers who use *parentese*—singsong, high-pitched talk—find that babies respond particularly happily to back-and-forth conversational turns. To do this, the caregiver should hold a baby securely under the bottom and under the head and put her face about eighteen inches from the baby's face. Talk with delighted tones, and use long, drawn-out vowels and short phrases: "Who's a pretty baby?" Parentese leads to a cascade of chemicals and electrical impulses flowing from baby's brain. The baby will thrust his legs out in delight at such appreciative talk and then will coo back. Waiting a turn, the adult can talk some more. A baby who experiences these talking turns during the early months soon becomes an eager participant in "conversations." The skilled adult partner knows how to wait for baby to vocalize back before continuing the leisurely conversation. The tuned-in adult also knows when to quit the conversation when the baby turns his head away signaling, "Okay, I have had a nice long talk, and now I need a rest!"

Most toddlers blossom forth with a vocabulary spurt after the middle of the second year. Then, single new words appear so frequently that an adult has a hard time trying to keep up with writing all of them down. Two-word phrases usually appear by the end of the second year as well. These phrases comprise many categories such as the following and other intriguing early word combinations (Honig, 2008):

- Possession: "My shoe"
- Commands: "Daddy fix!" or "Thtay dere!"
- Agent/action: "Doggy run!"
- Object/location: "Book table"
- Wishes: "Want dat!"
- Action/instrument: "Cut-knife"
- Questions: "Who dat?" or "Whazzat?"
- Object/description: "'tove hot"

Yet, some children are much slower to use *expressive language.* A perceptive caregiver will be particularly attuned to each child's *receptive language* ability. Receptive language, that is, what the child *understands,* is a better measure of whether a child is on track for language development. Children vary widely in how well they can articulate words. Some are reluctant to express themselves with words, particularly with new caregivers. If a child understands a great deal of what is said to him and is clearly able to follow simple activity directions, then the adult can keep on providing opportunities for rich turn-taking talk without worrying unduly about expressive language development, which has a wide window for development (Honig, 1996). Indeed, even some preschoolers with rich language still have trouble saying *bunny rabbit* and instead talk about the cute "wabbit."

The American Speech-Language-Hearing Association offers helpful information on children's language development, called How Does Your Child Hear and Talk? It is available at http://www.asha.org/public/speech/development/chart. htm.

Prerequisites for Developmental Advances

Caregivers need to consider physiological and physical developments that influence how and when learning milestones are reached. Development of muscular control proceeds from head to toe. Myelin, the white, fatty sheath that clothes neurons connected to muscles, must be fully developed before a child can control those muscles. Thus, tiny babies can coordinate their eye muscles early. Expertly, they move their eyes to look toward the door of the nursery when they hear a familiar voice calling out to them as they wake from a satisfying nap. Babies search for and then focus on that loving, familiar face. In contrast, myelin

sheaths that make wrist control and hand dexterity possible so that a toddler drinks juice expertly without spilling (mostly) may not be complete until nearly the end of the second year.

Toilet learning depends on full myelination of the long motor neurons that run down from the brain's motor cortex and supply the anal and urethral sphincters. When these neurons are fully sheathed in myelin, children can then voluntarily and quickly close and open those sphincter muscles. So, the skills for toilet learning depend not only on a toddler's patience for sitting on a potty, the ability to say the words *pee* and *poop*, or the ability to feel the inner bodily cues that urgently signal a need to go potty (Honig, 1993); myelination of those special neurons also has to be complete. To encourage parent patience and positive ways to promote a child's toilet learning, teachers can share this information with families who may devoutly wish for toddlers to be out of diapers.

Be aware of some children's special needs. If a child in the group was born prematurely, then some developmental milestones may be reached later than for others in the group. If a child has been shuttled from one foster home to another, again, this child may not meet developmental milestones when the others do. If a child has a disability such as autism, then certain social-emotional milestones in peer play may not be met at all in a timely manner. If a child is a recent immigrant or resides in a home where English is not spoken, then the child will surely struggle at first to cooperate with teacher instructions or to interact in creative peer play. Directors who share information with teachers will empower care providers in knowing when to wonder, when to give extra help, and when to ask for more help.

Knowledge of milestones for children with special needs is particularly important for a caregiver. Quality caregiving requires understanding not only of normative milestones but also of what is reasonable to expect for a child with special needs. Tuned-in teachers are sensitive to whether the window for each developmental accomplishment is narrow or wide and whether the child yet has the prerequisites in place for new learning. Knowing the prerequisites that undergird the development of each skill guides the caregiver in preparing for gradual learning and provision of just the right amount of support along the way. Caregivers adventurously use ingenuity and critical thinking about how and in what manner they can offer supports so that desired new behaviors are more likely to develop. Care providers use their perceptive skills to offer inviting activities that promote newly budding skills without undue child stress or anxiety.

> **Caregivers need to consider physiological and physical developments that influence how and when learning milestones are reached. Tuned-in teachers are sensitive to whether the window for each developmental accomplishment is narrow or wide and whether the child yet has the *prerequisites* in place for new learning.**

Creative thinking, planning, and activities that will enhance and advance a young child's development propel caregivers into a marvelous balancing act. A caregiver should not provide too much adult help, so that a child is not required to struggle at all to learn a new skill. Instead, a caregiver must provide sufficient encouragement to challenge the child himself to strive toward new learning. This is a challenge for new teachers and even for seasoned teachers! How can the caregiver provide sufficient adult supports so that the youngster who does make efforts to learn will feel the immense joy of new mastery? Consider the proud, thrown-back shoulders and wide smile of victory of a child who has just carefully wiggled a long metal chain vertically all the way down into the small opening of a box. How victorious he feels at his accomplishment!

A quality caregiver has to be an excellent detective. Adults have to know where a child is in terms of learning the prerequisites for a new skill, such as the wrist-turning ability that allows a child to place a puzzle piece correctly into its hole in the puzzle board. They also have to figure out what will be the optimal or personally more effective ways to support each child's early learning of a new skill. Should a teacher always just wait and watch to see how the child is doing on his own trying to wrestle with a new problem, such as stacking nesting blocks? Jean Piaget, the brilliant Swiss psychologist, affirmed that children must always construct new learning and new understanding on their own through personal experimentation with materials and interactions with peers. Yet, sometimes, if a particular child is easily discouraged at his first tries, a caregiver may decide quietly to provide unobtrusive help. She will support the elbow of that toddler struggling to stack nesting blocks. She will steady the lower blocks so a child can more readily continue to stack the upper blocks as he builds his tower.

Howard Gardner has advanced the theory of multiple intelligences. This suggests that children differ greatly in the domains of their skills and competencies. Thus, as children work at enhancing their skills and understandings, a quality caregiver carefully assesses each child's individual learning journey. The adult sets out to discover each child's passions and special gifts, as well as each child's frustration levels, and then can better make a decision about when and how to help.

Lev Vygotsky's idea of the zone of proximal development gives admirable affirmation to the teacher's subtle and essential role. The adult helps a child move from his current level of best performance to a slightly more advanced level. To use a metaphor: Teachers provide the supports, encouragement, and judiciously calibrated small steps whereby a child climbs higher on a learning ladder and moves to a higher level of task accomplishment. Teachers "lure" children into more and more successful and mature behaviors.

Emotional and Social Learning

To become an excellent detective and guide, a caregiver needs to know more than the developmental milestones that signify advances in a child's cognitive, language, fine-motor, and gross-motor learning. Just as promoting the development of intellect is important, and adults focus on activities to enhance IQ (intelligence quotient), so is the teacher actively engaged in promoting children's EQ (emotional quotient) (Goleman, 1995). Caregivers learn about the rich and complex world of a child's emotional and personality development so that they can better optimize the emotional well-being of young children. Teachers are in the forefront of helping children become able to focus on a task and to summon and use self-regulation techniques as they continue striving to solve a new and somewhat frustrating task. What emotional and personality aspects and emotional milestones are critical for caregivers to keep in mind?

Temperament Types

Children are born with a wide variety of temperament traits. Some are easy to soothe. The "easy" child persists longer at a challenging task. He may not respond as intensely when upset or distressed. When comforted, he may soon become able to play on his own with peers and toys.

Other children have fussy, more irritable, "triggery" temperaments. They get stressed more quickly when frustrated or angry. They may have more trouble settling after being comforted. Often they express intense reactions, whether joy or anger or sorrow. Helping the "feisty" child to feel less upset or indignant (when a toy is snatched by a peer, for example) may take far longer than with an "easy" child. Adults need insights into each child's temperament type. Caregivers need special reserves of patience and caring to soothe the feisty child when he is stressed and then need to devise ways to help that child move on to another interesting and satisfying activity.

The third temperament cluster is typical of the shy, slow-to-warm-up child. This child tends to withdraw from new foods, new caregivers, new routines, or even new arrangements of furniture in the classroom. Low-key moods and less predictable rhythms for daily naps, feedings, and toileting may be characteristic of this child. Activities that other children rush to participate in and explore with eagerness do not present the sense of a new adventure to a cautious child. Instead, "the new" represents a source of concern and wariness, even suspicion. With a shy or uncertain child, a caregiver needs to employ slow, soothing tones. The teacher needs to take the child's hand reassuringly and walk the child toward and settle the child into a new play situation rather than just say, "Go ahead, honey, and play with your friends with the train tracks over there!"

Mutuality in adult-child interactions is essential for emotionally satisfying outcomes (Erikson, 1950). Adult and child temperament types sometimes mesh harmoniously and sometimes cause miscommunications. How well a caregiver understands her own temperament type is as important as figuring out each child's main temperament traits (Honig, 1997b). Such awareness enhances a caregiver's insights in handling some perplexing emotional situations. A high-energy caregiver may enjoy a feisty child with intense and expressive feelings yet perhaps find it more difficult to slow down to engage the uncertain and cautious child, who might turn out to be quite enthusiastic after getting used to a new situation.

Tuning in to temperament is an important challenge for teachers. The adult can then better serve the needs of each child, particularly when a child is upset when urged to try new foods and activities or when encouraged to accept new persons when moved to another classroom in a child care center. Moving children to a new group together with their peers and friends increases child comfort and reduces the chances for child stress.

A caregiver's reassuring and sensitive attention to the needs of each child, regardless of temperament type, will create a harmonious spirit in the group. Indeed, when caregivers are attuned to temperament variations, they sometimes marvel at how cooperative and attentive a usually feisty child can act, for example, when snuggled next to a familiar teacher and sharing a lengthy and interesting picture story book.

Sensory Processing Troubles

Adults need to become aware of possible sensory processing and sensory integration difficulties a child may exhibit (Greenspan and Wieder, 2005). Some children cannot tolerate what they feel are "scratchy" clothes. They are only comfortable with soft cotton against their skin. Some children adore noisy romping times in a gym or outdoors. Others put their hands over their ears and retreat as far away as possible. One six-year-old climbed on top of all the mats in the gym to get away from the jumble of noise and kindergarten children jumping around. The teachers had a difficult time reaching him up there! He could not tolerate all the shrieking sounds of joyous peers at play. Some children are very sensitive to food textures. Others cannot bear if their peas touch the chicken on the lunch plate. Some babies get upset when you lay them down for a diaper change and get upset even when dry and clean and then picked up in arms; position change is uncomfortable. Some babies cannot stand light, feathery touches. That baby needs firm back pats and firm holding cheek-to-cheek as the caregiver hoists the baby for a walk around the room.

Young children with sensory integration troubles will be less frustrated when caregivers are aware of their needs and try to decrease sensory challenges so that the children feel less upset. Caregivers need to figure out when tastes, sounds, clothing type, or light touches seem to bother a particular child.

Stranger Anxiety

Temperament traits are not the only emotional cues that children give to a caregiver. Adults who care for infants also need to be aware of infant levels of stranger anxiety. Some babies react with extreme distress to new persons. This distress may start as early as six months and usually peaks between ten and eighteen months, as babies gradually gain the ability to learn to trust a variety of adults.

Enrollment in a new setting with strange adults and peers causes some babies to react with misery for weeks. These little ones need extra soothing and extra time in arms. Some children come from homes with language and culture customs different from those of classroom peers. Child anxiety may be eased if an adult sings soothing songs or murmurs some personal, loving words from the child's home language. Parents appreciate when a teacher calls on their personal expertise with the child, perhaps by asking for help in learning special loving words or an endearing nickname the family uses in the child's home language.

Secure Attachment Building

Babies usually develop their first secure attachment to the parent who provides tender, intimate care in everyday routine activities including feeding, bathing, dressing, cleaning, and settling to sleep. However, infants and young children may be in group care for long hours. Caregivers need to nourish a secure relationship between each little child and the care provider. Children flourish with adults who cherish them in intimate daily care experiences.

A child's early development attachment styles become part of an unconscious template for emotional styles with others as children grow up. Primary caregivers for infants and toddlers have more than a responsibility to help little ones to learn new cognitive and motor skills. Caregivers play the role of *emotional coaches.* Teachers nurture children who then gradually become securely attached, so that eventually youngsters learn to trust and learn from a wider range of adults invested in their welfare.

In their work, Mary Ainsworth and her colleagues have described four different attachment types:

- **Secure attachment:** A secure attachment between each child and the adult who is the cherishing caregiver should be the birthright of every child. Research in many nations shows that the majority (about two-thirds) of infants and young children are *securely emotionally attached* to one family adult or even several adults who provide tender, responsive care. The attuned adult who notices a baby's distress and who promptly meets the infant's needs with appropriate, sensitive caregiving responses, whether for a diaper change, a feeding, a cuddle, or a crooning lullaby, is helping that little one build a secure emotional relationship.

Caregivers notice when a child gladly greets her special adult at the end of a day. The child accepts cuddling and relaxes in a parent's or a grandparent's arms. When swept up for a reunion hug, the child enjoys the close contact and then is ready to get down and explore the environment. Ainsworth identified these babies as securely attached to the primary caregiver and also confirmed that secure attachment promoted child competence (Ainsworth, 1979; Ainsworth and Bell, 1974). When babies are securely attached by one year, researchers have confirmed that, a few years later, the children are more curious, more empathetic, and more sympathetic with peers and adults who act distressed; they are more self-directed and more competent. Some babies miss out. Stressed by harsh or insensitive caregiving over time, an infant may develop an insecure attachment. Based on pioneering work by John Bowlby and Mary Ainsworth, researchers have carefully noted three kinds of insecure attachment:

- **Insecure-avoidant attachment:** Some babies seem quite mature initially on entering and adjusting to child care. They ignore the parent's departure and do not seek reunion when she comes back. They may even run away to a far corner of the playroom or continue to play as if not noticing the adult who has come to take the child home. They seem to adjust so well to group care immediately. However, sometimes these babies have experienced care that was not attuned to their needs. The parent may be uncomfortable with close, loving bodily contact. The parent may be too stressed with job or personal troubles to tune into the distress signals the child sends when tired, wet, hungry, lonesome, or just needing some loving time. These babies have learned not to seek close contact from a parent.

■ **Insecure-ambivalent attachment:** Babies who have experienced inconsistent care are characterized as having insecure, hesitant, ambivalent attachments. They do seek out the parent for comfort when distressed. But, comfort has been provided only when the parent felt like it rather than when the child needed tender attentiveness, so this child may turn away after initially rushing for a hug at reunion time. The little one might even push at the adult and try to wiggle down from the adult's arms as if the child does not feel confident that this person will provide the reassurance or comfort so urgently sought.

■ **Dazed, disorganized attachment:** These children are characterized as exhibiting a mixture of behaviors observed for the other two insecure behavioral types. Sometimes these children have experienced abrupt or lengthy separation from parents. Sometimes the parents have been fearful and/or fear inducing with their children. Often such a child may exhibit confused behaviors. That child might run toward a familiar caregiver and then stop in his tracks as if he is not sure why he was going toward the person. The child may drift from one task to another. The child may not be able to look at the caregiver directly and may have stiff body posture if a caring adult tries to hold the little one on her lap. The child may reject a back rub and have a frightened look on his face.

Teachers may notice a variety of child responses to reunion times at the end of a child care day. Some children light up and run to a returning parent. Others burst into tears. This might be because seeing the beloved adult figure from whom separation has been so difficult causes a strong emotional reaction. These tears then may not be a sign of insecure attachment but of a child's strong emotions. Indeed, some parents complain that their little ones seem to "behave" so well in the child care setting and then act so "naughty" at home. Staff members need to reassure parents how important and special they are for their youngsters. Letting off steam, as it were, when safely back with the family may be a sign of a young child's trust in the bedrock foundation of acceptance and love the child feels from his family.

Gradually, teachers become aware of the quality of the attachment relationship between each little one and the adult family member who arrives with the child in the morning or who picks up that child at the end of the day. Some children cannot separate easily in the morning. They cling to the departing parent and refuse comfort. Since stranger anxiety is very intense in some infants, a baby with strong separation anxiety during the early weeks will need more holding in arms, more back rubs, and more tender and consoling murmured words until that baby learns that the caregiver too is a trustable and loving adult (Honig, 2002b).

Infant attachment styles often have long-term effects on later emotional and social behaviors of children. In one study, preschool children whose attachment styles had been carefully measured in infancy were brought into a preschool setting. Their experienced teachers had no clue as to the preschoolers' early attachment classifications. Yet, the children showed significant differences in the classroom in relationships with peers and teachers, and these differences were related to the children's early attachment ratings (Sroufe, 1983; Sroufe and Fleeson, 1986).

What this research revealed is quite troubling. Years after the infancy period, insecure early attachment patterns had important worrisome emotional consequences for preschoolers. Teachers treated with more indulgence those preschoolers who had been rated years before as insecure-ambivalent babies, and these children behaved in somewhat immature ways. Teachers tended more often to ignore those preschoolers who had been classified as securely attached in infancy. Teachers were the most controlling and disapproving with children who had been classified as insecure-avoidant in infancy.

When an insecure-avoidant preschooler was escorted with another preschooler into a separate playroom for a short play session, the insecure-avoidant child tended to bully a child who had been rated as insecure-ambivalently attached at one year of age. In turn, an insecure-ambivalent preschooler responded by *actively* assuming the role of victim with the bullying child! However, in contrast, when the insecure-avoidant child tried to bully a securely attached peer, the securely attached peer would simply move away and play alone with toys in that playroom. And, a securely attached youngster would play peacefully when paired with an insecure-ambivalent peer.

The need for at least one secure attachment to a cherishing adult is vital for emotional well-being throughout life. Child care teachers are in the front line of being able to provide each child with loving, tuned in, personally engaged experiences so that each child can develop a secure relationship with that adult. Day after day, such relationship building occurs during the innumerable acts of kindness

that teachers carry out during the course of their daily caregiving routines (Honig and Lally, 1981).

How young children are introduced into a child care situation may affect the quality of comfort they experience. Respectful and genuine staff interest in the parent and attentive approaches—welcoming words and gestures for the parents as well as the children—ease a child's transition to group care. Attentiveness by warm and caring teachers increases a child's feeling of comfort, even when parents, because of concern for their own work situation, feel that they cannot spend the extra time a teacher feels might help ease a young child's entry into a new care setting.

No matter what the child's attachment style may be, many young children do feel upset when left for long hours with adults who are, initially, strangers. In addition, even securely attached little ones tend to wilt toward the end of the day, just as flowers do after a long, hot day. Norwegian researchers in full-day centers with seasoned teachers observed that "tiredness in children seemed to accumulate during the week and reached its peak on Fridays" (Undheim and Drugli, 2012). Then, children needed more holding in arms or snuggly rocking-chair time.

When deciding optimal times to carry out an assessment of the quality of the relationship between care provider and child, directors often choose to wait several weeks after a child has been enrolled in care, to allow for adjustment time. Also, if children seem to become more upset at the end of long days in care, then the checklist preferably should be used for observations earlier in the day rather than late in the day. In any case, actively seek many and varied opportunities for assessment before making a decision about the quality of care a particular staff member provides.

PERSONAL INTERACTIONS: THE KEYS TO CARE QUALITY

In contrast to other measures that focus on a broader range of aspects of the total child care environment, the care quality checklist provides a specific focus on caregiver-child interactions and behaviors. When directors need to learn how effectively a caregiver is interacting to help each young child in her care flourish cognitively and emotionally, the checklist can be a helpful tool.

■ Director ratings can give teachers feedback on their practice of new skills.

■ Directors can use the information gained from the checklist to honor and appreciate the areas in which each caregiver is particularly adept.

■ Directors and mentor teachers can use the information to discover the domains of interpersonal interaction in which a caregiver might require further mentoring.

- Directors may learn of a specific teacher-child interaction area in which most staff could benefit from further learning opportunities. The director then may arrange for training opportunities to provide insights and skills in a specific area.
- The checklist can enhance a director's reflective supervision of staff.

Reflective supervision of staff has been found to reduce staff burnout and, as a consequence, to increase the chances for stability (rather than high turnover rates!) of caregiving staff. Stability and continuity are so necessary for adults to build trusting relationships with young children.

So, what exactly does quality care look like?

The Caregiver Is a Nourisher

Caring adults encourage the child in what Erik Erikson, the child-development theorist, calls *mutuality* in the relationship. A quality caregiver nourishes a child's fundamental feeling of being lovable and provides tuned-in companionship for each of the children in care.

For some little ones, separation anxiety may be high; some children become intensely upset when their family members leave in the morning. During the first days and weeks in a new care setting, that child may need special help to feel at ease. A caregiver who uses personalized, reassuring voice tones and finds ways to provide interesting opportunities for one-on-one quiet play with toys that absorb the child's interest shows devotion and wisdom in choosing intimate, loving ways to guide each child toward feeling comfortable and secure in group care.

Cortisol, a stress hormone, rises during the day from morning to afternoon while a child is in group care, but the hormone does not rise when the child is at home, such as during a weekend (Vermeer and van IJzendoorn, 2006). Thus, even a child who appears to show no separation anxiety by crying or looking worried or sad may still be feeling stress. Research also has shown that the rise in cortisol is greater when children are experiencing conflicted relationships with their teachers (Lisonbee et al., 2008). The quality of teacher interactions is particularly crucial to decrease child stress. The nourishing adult makes sure each child is warmly welcomed and feels comfortable in the child care setting. Particularly for infants and toddlers, freely available lap time is important. During the first weeks in care, cuddling and holding may be just what a baby needs to feel secure.

Personalized care is especially important if a child has heightened stranger anxiety. This natural worry about strangers often occurs when babies under one year old are initially left in the care of others. Babies worry as they look at unfamiliar faces and are held in arms and ministered to by hands that do not feel familiar. For some babies, these new experiences feel stressful for many weeks.

Calm tempos help all children gradually feel comfortable in a new environment. With the youngest children, caregivers use caresses; smiles; soothing gestures; and slow, leisurely motions to reassure little ones. Brief, daily massages with nonallergenic oils help many babies relax into calm, serene adjustments to nonparental care.

Calm tempos **help all children gradually feel comfortable in a new environment.**

A young child who sighs contentedly and molds onto the new caregiver's body, whose face brightens up, and who reaches out to be picked up when the caregiver comes back into the room after a short break is showing how much trust has been built between the child and the caregiver.

If a child lives in a family that speaks a language other than English, the nourishing provider asks the parent to teach him a few tender words in that child's language to soothe and comfort the child. Learning some simple lullabies or easy songs in the child's home language often reassures a child that the group setting is just homey enough to enable the child to relax and enjoy peer experiences. The familiar songs and words help the child trust that the caregiver is available if the child feels lonely, upset, tired, or just needs some snuggle time.

A trusted caregiver serves as a child's refueling station, where a child can go to restore energy and then cope with life's challenges (Kaplan, 1978). A child seeks a refueling adult, for example, if the child feels frustrated. Perhaps the Lego bricks she was playing with did not hold together when she tried her own design. Perhaps he became upset when his carefully arranged block tower was knocked down by an enthusiastic peer galloping across the room. The caregiver's physical availability and soothing, encouraging words provide comfort.

The nourishing caregiver shines loving eyes at a child and provides smiles of encouragement and admiration that spread feelings of well-being and of being lovable through a child's whole body. The young child who has a secure attachment to her primary caregiver seems to sink into a feeling of somatic certainty and peacefulness when held by the caregiver. That child is fortunate! She has not only a loving, secure attachment with each cherishing family member but also a secure attachment to another special adult. Secure attachment during the early years is a powerful predictor of a child's ability to make friends more easily, to be sociable, empathetic, and caring toward others years later (Honig, 2002b). Fortunately, a child is capable of developing trust and a uniquely positive attachment to each of several adult attachment figures—parents, grandparents, and caregivers.

Adults who trust themselves to be loving and facilitative are sensitive to the child's signals of distress and responsive to expressed needs. Attachment researchers have confirmed how crucial it is for caregivers to provide assurance that a child is well-loved through daily tuned-in, intimate ministrations. A quality caregiver nurtures each child's trust in the adult and acknowledges the child's own ability to express distress and to get someone to meet those needs promptly and effectively. Trust is built on a four-way signal system:

■ The child trusts himself: "When I am feeling miserable, I can cry really loud!"

■ The child trusts the willingness and efficacy of the caregiver to fix the problem.

■ The caregiver trusts her own effectiveness.

■ The caregiver acknowledges and attends promptly and appropriately to the child's signals of stress or distress. (Honig, 2011)

The emotional curriculum of a quality child care program advances a child's development when all those four signals are Go! The nourishing caregiver shares joy and tenderness while providing deeply affirmative care.

- The teacher's voice tones are positive and genuinely caressing.
- The teacher frequently and generously provides lap and snuggling times.
- The adult gets down on the floor with young children and plays with them.
- The caregiver rubs the backs of children at nap time and/or uses a rocking chair to settle and soothe a fretful child.
- The teacher conscientiously attends to the children's safety, health, and physical well-being.

The Caregiver Is a Good Classroom Arranger

Teachers report that the richer the varieties of experience available to children, the more interesting the explorations the children undertake and the less conflict among the children. A nurturing, thoughtful caregiver will consider ways to meet the needs of the children in her care and will provide opportunities and spaces for boisterous play and for quieter exploration.

Highly active children need to run, climb, and use their muscles. Less active children may prefer to curl up in a cozy corner with a favorite picture book—some have even memorized the rhymes of Dr. Seuss's *The Cat in the Hat* and can recite them to themselves at four years of age!

The caregiver provides opportunities for lots of physical movement. He offers a rocking horse, tricycles, and outdoor play spaces or indoor gym spaces where children can let off steam as well as hone their large- and small-muscle skills.

Within a room arranged and marked so that the children can clearly understand the purpose for each space, the teacher can spend more time interacting one-on-one with the children. She can check in with the children individually, seeking to understand their explorations and sharing in their discoveries.

The Project Approach, described by Dr. Lilian Katz, extends preschoolers' interests over time as they work at joint cooperative activities. One project she describes involved taking a group of preschoolers to visit an automotive repair shop lab. When back in the classroom, the teachers took pleasure in watching how children's creativity and zestful enthusiasm resulted in their determination and efforts to create an auto repair shop of their own, with cardboard and found materials.

Projects provide children with the challenges and rewards of an extended joint exploration together. A visit to a restaurant may inspire children to create their own food service place in the classroom—complete with taking orders earnestly scribbled on notepads, creating menus with teacher help, and using playdough to create tasty "foods" for peers who play customers. Teachers need to encourage sustained child enthusiasm for such projects.

A project can also involve cooperative artwork. A project could be working together to draw a mural of the sea on a long paper tacked to a classroom wall. Children can contribute their drawings or paintings of dancing blue waves, fishing boats, tug boats, whales, fishes, and other sea creatures as well as seashells on the sandy bottom.

Children who more frequently choose to use open-ended materials upon which they can impose their own goals and ideals can make more cognitive gains than children who most frequently play with closed-ended materials. Make *both* kinds of materials available to children. Closed-ended materials, such as pegboards or puzzles, have a clear goal. Open-ended materials, such as large building blocks, playdough, or a dress-up corner with lots of different outfits and accessories, offer the children a myriad of ways to explore and imagine. Play with a rich variety of materials and with peers enhances children's skills and creativity and also sustains their desire for extending play in more complex ways (Honig, 2001b; 2007). As Alison Gopnik has forthrightly affirmed, "Play is a crucial part of what makes all humans so smart." Teacher preparation can increase children's opportunities for rich play experiences that facilitate early learning.

○ The caregiver provides opportunities for the children to use open-ended materials as well as closed-ended materials.

○ The caregiver provides areas where children can safely play with water in tubs with different floatable and sinkable toys.

○ The caregiver provides areas where children can play with dry materials, such as tubs filled with rice or sand, with different small toys hidden inside.

○ The caregiver provides opportunities for vigorous movement and large-muscle activity.

○ The caregiver provides areas, work centers, or tables where children can practice small-muscle skills with appropriate materials.

○ The caregiver offers a cool-off corner or a "thinking-chair," safely within view of the teacher, where an overstimulated child can calm down.

○ The caregiver arranges room dividers and furniture so that attractive learning centers are available and marked so that children clearly can understand the uses for each area.

The Room where the Children Are Cared for Seems Harmonious and Aesthetically Lovely to Live In

Aesthetics are important for young children. When adults provide peaceful, attractive settings that are uncluttered and filled with interesting work and play areas, children enjoy learning while living in beautiful spaces. Some artistic parents, if teachers ask, may be willing to create colorful banners to hang on the walls. Fronds could sway in the breeze when spider plants and other greenery are hung from the ceiling. White narcissus bulbs planted in bowls with water and pebbles will produce flowers that perfume the room and provide visual pleasure. Inexpensive posters of paintings by Renoir, Monet, Cassatt, or other artists can provide inexpensive models of fine art for young children. Displaying photos of the children interacting with family members and displaying personal items, such as cultural elements from each family, affirms for children that their teacher cares about their families' activities.

○ The caregiver arranges the environment for harmonious child interactions, for enhancing children's aesthetic sense of beauty and loveliness.
○ The caregiver incorporates photos and other elements sent from children's homes to give a personal feel to the space.

The Caregiver Is a Good Observer

A quality caregiver needs subtle and sophisticated child-watching skills. Such skills help us to tune in to and keep an eye on what and how and with whom events are happening. A quality caregiver particularly needs to watch body language, such as a scowling forehead, clenched fists, a tired shoulder droop, or eyes that avoid contact. Child watching provides thrills for caregivers when they tune in to small signs of more mature behaviors or social skills. Teachers are likely to experience deep personal satisfaction when a child is indeed thriving in their care, and this can ensure less burnout and a greater chance that a teacher will stay in the profession, a situation that many directors devoutly hope for.

Some children find being sociable easy. Others hang at the fringes of a play activity without knowing how to enter into play with peers. Teachers who observe carefully can often devise ways to assist each child toward optimizing skills and abilities. For example, suppose a group of preschoolers is playing house in the housekeeping corner. Troy is longing to enter their play, but they tell him they have a daddy and a mommy and kids already. The creative teacher can cheerfully suggest that maybe Troy can be the postman bringing some special delivery packages (perhaps birthday presents!) to the family. They will need to sign or scribble their names to make sure that the post office knows that they have received their packages. The family can celebrate receiving the packages by inviting Troy in to share some treats with them.

A caregiver needs to interpret child behaviors as accurately as possible. Sometimes watching a child carefully as he interacts with peers or with gooey materials, when asked to climb steep steps, or when asked to solve a slightly difficult puzzle provides special insights for the caring adult. The teacher will be able to more deftly confirm and support a child's special interests or ease another child's particular worries or fear.

Individual children have different and varied interests. Some are fascinated by tadpoles, gerbils, or ants busy at work in the grass. Some adore trucks and cars with a passion. Some love to dress up dollies and teddies and pretend to feed them and settle them in toy cribs for naps. Children relish the chance to run and jump and use their large muscles in almost perpetual motion. Some are fascinated by animals and fearlessly delight in petting or hugging even a large dog. Yet, another child acts frightened by a puppy's enthusiastic licks and joyous antics.

Some children prefer to hammer and build. Young friends in the group love to dress up in firefighter helmets and pretend to put out fires and do other heroic deeds. Some are intensely curious about earthworms or bugs such as grasshoppers, spotted ladybugs, or butterflies. Children love to collect stuff, whether leaves on the ground, bottle caps, rocks, or other nature bits, including dandelions that, alas, do wilt fast when clutched in a little fist and saved as gifts for parents.

○ The caregiver observes children's body language and finds caring ways to ease fears or encourage the frustrated child.
○ The caregiver uses creative and positive ways to help less socially adept children enter into playgroups with peers.
○ The caregiver notices children's interests and preferences and capitalizes on them by providing materials and props to facilitate complex play and pretend play experiences.

The Caregiver Encourages Competency at Everyday Personal Tasks

Long-term observation in families has shown that, by age three, well-developing children can be distinguished from less competent youngsters. In the case of more competent preschoolers, family interactions involve much language and rich opportunities for learning. When children are invited to participate in daily routines, such as meal times, clean-up times, and planning times, they increase their competency skills and self-confidence.

Every time a child helps with a task or shows initiative, a caregiver can use words to note that specifically: "You set out one spoon and one paper plate for each child for snack time. Thank you, Sam. That was such careful setting the table. You are such a good helper." Provide words parallel to a child's positive actions; for example, offer an appreciative and admiring tone as a child tries a new and difficult task or acts more patiently or less impulsively and is able to use words instead of aggressive actions right away.

At the water table, Ofira is thrusting out her tongue as a sign of her strenuous effort to pour water carefully from one cup to a deeper cup with a narrower mouth. She focuses intently and pours while steadying each hand performing a separate task, a technique called *hold and operate.* Her teacher praises her using the words *carefully* and *slowly* in a positive tone.

This dexterity practice is useful for a host of other skills, such as sharpening a pencil by holding the pencil steady with one hand and turning the handle with the other, or turning an eggbeater in making scrambled eggs, or turning a drawer handle to slide open a drawer and neatly put away the toys the child is holding with her other hand.

○ The caregiver encourages children to help set out utensils and napkins before a meal.

○ The caregiver encourages children to help in clearing dishes and utensils after the meal.

○ The caregiver encourages self-care with shoes and coats and provides painting smocks that are easy to fasten and put on with minimal adult help.

○ The caregiver offers specific praise and encouragement to children as they attempt everyday tasks.

The Caregiver Boosts Thinking and Reasoning Skills

Jean Piaget, the Swiss psychologist, taught that a young child constructs his ideas of how the world works and what physical and social realities are from his experiences interacting with materials and with peers. Children learn as they grapple adventurously with toys or events that challenge their current understandings: A young child sees a pile of potatoes on the kitchen counter, reaches for one, tries to bounce the potato, and then reacts with amazement when this round, brown item that looks like a ball does not bounce at all.

During the preschool period, children learn about grouping items, identifying and sorting materials (Honig, 1982). Early on, they learn the names for parts of the body. Teachers point out that vehicles include cars, trucks, trains, buses, bikes, scooters, and motorcycles. Furniture includes tables, chairs, couches, stools, hutches, lounge chairs, divans, hassocks, and so on. Classification skills increase children's concept learning. The ability to sort and classify helps children clarify their own ideas about how the world of living creatures and nonliving items is organized.

Learning to sort by color, shape, size, and even to sort items by looking for two simultaneous attributes, such as same color *and* size, is an important preschool learning challenge. Children also learn to order items and attributes by qualities, such as bigger and smaller, heavier and lighter, smoother and rougher, longer and shorter, or happier and sadder. Some of these polar opposites, such as shallow versus deep (Honig, 1996), are still difficult even for five-year-olds.

They can find shapes that match each other. Preparing and setting out three-dimensional materials boosts younger children's ability to learn to make successful matches. Preschoolers are challenged by the more difficult task of searching among two-dimensional pictured items for examples of shapes that differ only in size or in color.

At clean-up time, children learn to sort items they have been using in play. Toy animals get put together on one shelf, trucks and cars in a different space. Children need lots of experience with materials and a boost from a caregiver who makes a judicious remark or an encouraging suggestion at the right time. Successful task solutions increase children's confidence in their ability to succeed at learning tasks. With their thoughtful planning, teachers make children's cognitive accomplishments possible.

Planning is also required to assist children in learning early math skills. Preschoolers need opportunities to estimate and count single objects. In a simple linear number board game, for example, preschoolers from low-income families were shown how to roll dice and then advance a little counter on the game board by counting out loud the number of boxes designated by their dice roll. After playing the game, they improved significantly in counting skills (Siegler, 2010).

Suppose at snack time a child indignantly complains that another child "has more cookies than me!" An adult can point out that the child has more pieces of cookie because he broke his cookie into chunks to eat, and all together he has just as much cookie to eat as the complaining peer. Number sense and amount are important concepts for preschoolers to learn. Piaget noted that as children work with materials, they construct *logico-mathematical knowledge* of the world. They learn that no matter whether a teacher pours juice from a pitcher into many smaller cups or into only two larger cups, the amount of juice has not changed. A preschooler learns that, no matter whether she arranges a bunch of small items so that they touch each other in a circle or spreads them out in a long line on a table, there will still be the same number of items. The more such experiences a preschooler has, the more the child comes to understand that number and amount do not depend on placement of objects but on counting one item at a time. This is important mathematical learning!

Cooking activities are attractive ways for preschoolers to learn material transformations. Budding scientists, they see before their eyes that goopy, liquid, raw eggs, cooked in an electric fry pan, turn into solid scrambled eggs. Stirring with a spoon, they notice that sugar dissolves and disappears in a cup of water. Work with a toy eggbeater provides knowledge of transformations as well as increases wrist dexterity. Preschoolers whip liquid heavy cream in a bowl and watch it finally turn into soft but solid butter. Pouring grains of powder from an instant pudding package into a bowl with milk, they use an eggbeater and find out that the whipped liquid turns into a smooth dessert of firm consistency (Blank, 1975). Watching as a faucet is turned off slowly, children notice that the stream of water turns into drips. Amazing! The child whose scientific curiosity is nurtured will ask the caregiver zillions of questions!

○ The caregiver helps the child reason, analyze, search, sort, and think of explanations for sorting in certain ways.

○ The caregiver provides safe and supervised meal-preparation opportunities for young children to learn transformations.

○ The caregiver encourages the child to make shrewd, reasonable guesses: "What will happen if…?"

○ The caregiver provides opportunities for counting individual items and making numerical estimates.

○ The caregiver teaches concepts such as opposites in a positive way.

The Caregiver Is a Good "Matchmaker"

Using their perceptive noticing skills, caregivers tune in to each child's gifts and strengths. Teachers set reasonable learning goals, arrange materials, and offer experiences for discoveries that are neither too easy nor too difficult for each child. Adults need to choose activities that will be a bit challenging, intriguing, and a little difficult to learn. Piagetian theory and lots of classroom experience with learners at different levels reveal that learning takes place when there is a good match between where the child is developmentally and new learning that is just somewhat challenging or different. Challenges that are too strange or complicated can discourage a child, making her feel angry and frustrated. A quality caregiver matches experiences, suggestions, questions, and information to the level where each child can currently handle the ideas or actions involved. Developmental psychologist Lev Vygotsky calls this the *zone of proximal development*.

When working with a child to advance learning, the teacher's role is centrally important. She lures the child into more venturesome tries, more advanced understandings, and greater skill in problem solving. When the caregiver is a perceptive, accurate matchmaker, then a child's pleasure in learning and active pursuit of accomplishment will unfold right before a teacher's eyes!

○ The caregiver shows awareness of and adjusts for the level of difficulty of a task when working with the individual child or with the group.
○ The caregiver prepares materials slightly varied in difficulty before beginning an activity, to ensure that there will be an appropriate match for each child.

The Caregiver Encourages Creativity and Pretend Play

Young children are attuned to and respond with joy to beauty. After a rainstorm, a toddler in an adult's arms watches wide-eyed at the window as a colorful rainbow arcs across the sky. Wrinkling their noses with pleasure, little children sniff perfumed flowers, such as hyacinths.

Music invites children to dance and sway and twirl. Songs such as "The Wheels on the Bus," chants such as "Five Little Monkeys Jumping on a Bed," and fingerplays such as "The Itsy Bitsy Spider" spark children's enthusiasm for learning songs, chants, and the hand and body movements that accompany them (Honig, 1995). Songs also help preschoolers learn rhyme schemes, an important skill for flourishing language.

Nurturing a child's creativity, a caregiver increases a child's innate wonder in discovering aesthetic delights. Children are fascinated by the flick of a goldfish's tail in a tank in the classroom. They react with happiness as they watch baby birds that have hatched in a nest in a tree outside the classroom window. They comment excitedly on the devoted ways in which parent birds bring food for the baby birds. Eventually, the children experience the special delight of seeing the little birds fledge and fly away.

Play is the living theater in which young children learn about the amazing new world whose sights, sounds, textures, rules, tastes, and other pleasures they are just beginning to navigate, and in which they must find their special ways and place.

How does play support early learning? Children learn how their bodies move. Listening to soft waltz music, a toddler clutches a gauzy piece of nylon and twirls his body round and round. Lying stretched out in front of a mirror anchored firmly at floor level, another toddler stretches her body and twists and turns while watching her reflection as she plays at switching to different positions. Holding each other's ankles, toddlers pretend they are snakes and slither across the playroom floor while vocalizing their own version of hissing sounds. As their teacher reads a book about rabbits, some tots start hop-hop-hopping around as they hear the word *hop.* Through participation in fingerplays, children develop their fine-motor skills, watching closely and copying the gestures that go with the songs.

Through play, children learn what a toy can do and learn what they can do with a toy. During sensorimotor play, babies learn the properties of different materials. To his surprise, a baby finds that a colorful wooden block he is mouthing has hard corners, not at all like the soft chewy foods he enjoys. How different the texture feels compared with the soft blanket he strokes gently while sucking his thumb and settling into slumber. Put a rattle in a baby's hand and she will experiment. She brings it to eye level. She bangs it on her high-chair table. She tries chewing it but cannot fit that big thing in her mouth. She tries shaking the rattle, and she is surprised at the nice sound it makes. Shaking vigorously and then also more gently she experiments with making louder and softer sounds and increases her wrist control as well as her feeling of competence at her ability to produce the sounds.

Play encourages mastery. A baby places a big block over and over on top of a smaller block. The top block keeps toppling over and falling onto the table. Frustrating! After watching this scenario for a while, the teacher takes two blocks from the table and plays alongside the baby. She places a small block on top of a bigger block and in a singsong voice chants, "On top, on top. Little block goes on top!" The baby notices and then tries this way. Happily, the little block stays on the big block, and the baby is able to stack a few more blocks to make a tower. More play with blocks, increasing hand dexterity, and careful attention will help the baby to learn to line the edges up so the blocks do not topple over. The child is on his way toward mastering tower building with blocks. A few years later, towers, castles, and fancy structures will attest to the blossoming building power made possible through extended play with blocks.

Children creatively learn to substitute one object for another. Providing time, space, and props for play encourages creative mental representations. For example, taking a large clam shell from the science table, an older toddler seats his teddy bear on the big shell and firmly announces, "Teddy go potty!" This youngster is able to visualize the shell as a potty for his teddy bear.

Solitary play can help little ones investigate a toy thoroughly and may strengthen concentration skills and persistence. For example, although other babies and toddlers are on the rug in her vicinity, a child concentrates on turning the large toy egg timer up and down. Carefully she tracks with her eyes how the sand slowly empties out of the top part. Then, she flips the toy over and again watches carefully as the sand pours downward. Gravity is a mystery. She is not distracted by other children's noises.

Parallel play helps young toddlers feel comfortable with peers in their earliest social togetherness. As two toddlers play side by side, it might seem as if they are not paying any attention to one another. Seated in the sandbox, each is making a mud pie with sand and water and then turning the pail upside down to pour out the "pie." However, as soon as one toddler gets up to leave, the other loses interest in her play, too. They had been quietly enjoying their side-by-side play.

Pretend play with peers enriches social skills. Pretend social play offers toddlers a chance to use and expand imagination and to replay scenes from home life or from other experiences. For example, after the terrible destruction of the Twin Towers on September 11, 2001, I watched young children in child care play at pretend bombing. They flew toy airplanes over and over to knock down a tower of blocks. By re-enacting the destruction, the children gained some control over the tragic scenes they had watched on television. A teacher' sympathetic guidance and support can allow for safe play that helps a child gain control over scary feelings. Children often act out play roles with great earnestness. They don firefighter slickers and pretend to put out fires and save people in burning buildings. As Klugman and Smilansky (1990) state, children pretend to play doctor, explorer, or superhero. Make believe with objects enhances their cognitive ability and creativity.

The more varied the props that adults provide, the greater the possibilities for creative pretend play. Children put on dress-up clothes and take on many different roles. At the lunch table, a child has munched on several carrot sticks. Then, with a sparkling smile, she picks up a carrot stick, swipes it across her brow, and announces, "I's doing my eyebrows." What a creative symbolic gesture!

Play provides a chance to negotiate peer conflicts. Toddlers who engage in social pretend play will invariably need to negotiate personal differences in the scenarios they create. "You be the mommy, and I'll be the daddy," announces a boy. What if his friend wants to be the daddy? Can they decide to take turns? How can they find a way to keep playing and work out their different wishes? A teacher can help little ones learn that they can agree with each other's plans some of the time but not all of the time (Shure, 1996).

While watching her little ones dig in the dirt outside, a caregiver hears a child call out, "I making you a cake, Teacher!"

"What kind of cake?" she asks.

"A chocolate cake," she replies, beaming as she looks down at the brown earth she is digging.

"Oh, yummy. I love chocolate cake," answers her teacher.

Such small, intimate interactions nurture a child's imaginary play and creative abilities.

Peer-group entry skills are sometimes in short supply in young children. Some children need help in developing peer-play skills. Perhaps they need help to find words or gestures to invite themselves into a group. By facilitating peer play, a caregiver can guide a cautious or withdrawn child to find ways to interact pleasurably with peers (Honig and Thompson, 1994). Learning how to enter a playgroup is not easy for shy children. But, temperament is not destiny (Honig, 2002b). Thoughtfully, gently, creatively, a caregiver can promote a child's entry into a peer activity. Noticing a little one's longing look, her caregiver calls out, "José, you are having such fun pulling your wagon and giving your teddy bear a ride around the room. Charlene is hoping that you can take her teddy for a ride, too!" Charlene smiles shyly as José stops his wagon and invites her teddy for a ride.

Noticing that one of his toddlers has not yet learned to pretend, Mr. Richard calls out as a boy approaches, lugging blocks of different sizes and shapes in his wagon. "I need to buy some strawberries. Do you have some red strawberries, Hoagy? The child stops and looks up very puzzled at his teacher. Mr. Richard picks up two small, red blocks and says, "These look like nice, yummy, red strawberries. How much do you charge for two of them?" The first go-round, the child seems bewildered, but by the second and third time he drags his wagon around, he stops at his teacher almost expecting that he would want to "buy" some carrots (orange blocks) or some blueberries (blue blocks). Thus, in that one small, personal interaction, Mr. Richard helps Hoagy enter the enjoyable world of pretend play and earn some imaginary money, too!

Play promotes cognitive skills. If one child in group play is puzzled about how the play can continue, a peer may suggest a useful idea or may lug over a prop that can substitute for the missing play object they need. For example, children need to measure a box big enough for all the stuff they want to put inside or they need to see which train track will fit around a curve rather than straight ahead. Math and measuring skills, as well as thinking and reasoning skills, are all rooted in the generous play time teachers provide for the children in their care. Social pretend play scenarios evoke children's thinking skills as they immerse themselves in their small dramas (Saracho and Spodek, 1998).

○ The caregiver provides rhythmic, musical, and chanting experiences.

○ The caregiver encourages the children to use their bodies expressively in dance, drama, costume, and movement.

○ The caregiver sets up a dress-up area with clothes that are appealing for boys and girls.

○ The caregiver provides large cartons and other props to encourage pretend play.

○ The caregiver actively promotes children's role-play abilities and imaginative games.

The Caregiver Provides Positive Contingent Reinforcement

Building up children's prosocial actions is an important teacher task. To boost children's positive behaviors toward goals, a caregiver needs to reward desired behaviors and, whenever possible, to ignore more immature or inappropriate behaviors. Of course, adults cannot permit aggressive actions; they should use firm, calm ways to stop aggression. Positive contingent reinforcement (PCR) means that teachers give children prompt attention and positive feedback when the children are behaving appropriately or acting in ways that are developmentally desirable. The "prompt" part is important. When used with deliberate planning, PCR will result in fewer difficult episodes when a frazzled caregiver simply reacts to frustrating events in the room by nagging or by blurting out frequent *no-nos*.

Behaviors become more positive as adults emphasize a child's strengths and appropriate behaviors rather than dwell on disapproved aspects of behavior. A caregiver needs to stress the things he admires in a child—even a child who is a slower learner or who causes more than her share of upsets at the center. An ingenious caregiver uses PCR honestly and accurately in every aspect of daily life in group care.

○ The caregiver provides positive, clear, contingent reinforcement.
○ The caregiver ignores, as much as possible, immature or inappropriate behaviors.

The Caregiver Is a Language Enlarger

Quality caregivers promote language with precision, passion, and pleasure (Honig and Brophy, 1996). The number of different words a caregiver uses is important, as new words stretch children's vocabularies. Even when a toddler does not recognize a new word, a teacher can help that little one learn the word quickly. For example, in an experiment, a teacher sets a toy doggie, a toy car, and a toy cup on the tabletop along with a strange new object—a toy eggbeater. First, the teacher says to a child, "Please give me the doggy," and then thanks the little one and returns that toy to its place. Next, the teacher says, "Please give me the dax." The toddler, familiar with the other toys, quickly realizes that *dax* must be the name of the new toy and hands the toy eggbeater to the teacher. This is a way children recognize new words, as shown in reserach by Markman and Hutchinson. Nouns are easier than verbs for them, so be sure to say the name of every toy, person, color, clothing item, or body part, as well as colors, shapes, and actions, such as jumping, reaching, smiling, or waving bye-bye.

The frequency, richness, and responsiveness of language interactions differ very much among families. Hart and Risley (1999) observed young children at home with their families. Their research revealed that parents with less education talked far less with their children as compared with more educated parents. These toddlers' language skills lagged behind those of children from families with higher education. By early grade school, the vocabulary differences were immense. Children from educated families had thousands more words in their vocabularies.

In England, Joan Tough recorded three-year-olds playing outdoors on the center playground with their friends. She reported her findings in her book *The Development of Meaning: A Study of Children's Use of Language*. Compared with children from more educated families, she found significant differences in language skills:

> Children from less-advantaged families were not using language spontaneously...for recalling and giving details of past experience; reasoning about present and recalled experience; anticipating future events and predicting the outcome; recognizing and offering solutions to problems; planning and surveying alternatives for possible courses of action; projecting into the experiences and feelings of other people; using the imagination to build scenes through the use of language for their play.

Talking with young children is crucial! Varying their voice tones while talking, teachers arouse and galvanize children's curiosity and interest. Quality caregivers extend conversations with young children, show genuine interest in their talk together, and give children time to find words to express their ideas and feelings (Honig, 2008). Outside on the playground, adults need to stay alert to how much they are talking with children rather than with other caregivers (Tizard, Cooperman, Joseph, and Tizard, 1972). Caregivers can use words to promote peer cooperation outdoors as well as during indoor play. Opportunities abound outdoors for teachers to label actions, goals, and all sorts of activities. Taking a walk in nature, teachers nurture children's curiosity and noticing skills by providing names for plants, flowers, rocks, insects, and birds that fascinate children.

In building on language-enriching opportunities, caregivers will find several principles useful.

- **Matchmaking:** Because children have quite varied interests, teachers need to find ways to enhance a child's language repertoire in the special area of each child's interest, whether zoo animals, plumbing pipes, pond creatures, or football scores. Teachers should speak so that children can understand the message. Familiar words and sounds reassure a child. An adult talking too fast or in phrases too complicated for a particular child's level of understanding may dampen that child's willingness to try to communicate with language.

- **Positive contingent reinforcement:** Express pleasure in children's language understandings and in children's talk. Converse with children. Expand on their brief remarks. Clarity and simplicity in talk and explanations help children understand more of what an adult is trying to communicate.

- **Self-talk:** Teachers need to talk as they do things with and for children: "Glen, you chose red paint. So, I am carefully pouring some red paint into a little cup for you to use at the easel for your painting," or "We have six children who will eat snack. We will need six napkins: one, two, three . . ."
- **Parallel talk:** The caregiver labels objects, talks about what a child is doing, and clarifies a child's feelings by using descriptive words: "Naftali, you and Ofira are working so carefully together to create a long set of tracks for your cars to travel on. You both make a fine team working together" (Honig, 2001a).

Creative language promoters use the varied occasions and circumstances of the child care environment and their own daily routines to enlarge children's language repertoires (Jalongo, 2007). The diapering table is a great place to talk with each individual infant or toddler. Preschoolers may clamor to share important information about events and styles of action that have occurred at home or on a weekend family excursion. A language-promoting caregiver enjoys and appreciates when children talk about and share family experiences with each other, such as at the lunch table when a child informs the group, "My mama serves hot dogs with mustard AND ketchup AND frijoles!" In the morning, many preschoolers enjoy sharing their dreams (and sometimes nightmares, too) from the night before; this can be an important sharing time, as about a quarter of male children report that monsters feature in many dreams (Honig and Nealis, 2011).

A perceptive caregiver will use language expressively and frequently when a child seems to have delayed language skills. Teachers try different voice registers and change voice tones. They simplify speech when necessary. Adult types of talk will vary sensitively, depending on a child's stage of development and degree of communication competence. Adults vary their communications by emphasis, simplifications, intonations, and pitch to engage young children's interest in conversations and storytelling.

Sometimes a caregiver, without meaning to, discourages a young child or squashes early competency in labeling. The caregiver might say, for example, to a toddler who confidently calls a pictured bus a *truck:* "Oh no, that's not a truck!" Instead, the caregiver could remark, "This bus looks somewhat like a truck. A truck and a bus both do have a driver. But let's look at the passengers sitting *inside* the bus. A big bus takes people where they want to go. A truck carries stuff that people and stores need, such as food or furniture or televisions."

Teachers introduce concepts such as *same* and *different.* The teacher helps children focus on details that will enhance further learning. Adults encourage children to explain to the teacher; for example, a teacher may comment, "LaToya, I love all the blue, blue paint you have been using for your painting. Can you tell me something about your picture?"

Very young children tackle learning to ask and answer who, what, how, where, and how much questions. Toddlers may also ask why, but they have only a vague idea of what an appropriate answer might be. Toddlers sometimes ask absurd why questions such as, "Why the garage door?" that an adult would be hard put to decipher, much less answer! Research has shown that the vast majority (80 percent) of questions teachers ask young children are convergent questions (questions with only one answer), such as, "Do you need to go potty?" "What color is this flower?" "Who is looking for his ball in the bushes in this picture?" (Wittmer and Honig, 1991).

Children's responses to adult Socratic, open-ended questions help a teacher figure out how children are reasoning, recalling events from memory, and sequencing thoughts. A personal example:

> Seeing my colorful print dress with elephant designs, a three-year-old looked carefully and then assured me: "Them's elephants!"
>
> "How can you tell?" I asked the child while giving him my full attention.
>
> With assurance and bodily acting out by lifting his feet in turn, ponderously swaying from side to side, the preschooler earnestly explained to me: "'Cause them gots big feet that go boom, boom, boom!" (Honig, 1996)

Open-ended, Socratic questions stimulate children to think deeply. These questions challenge children to retrieve information from memory and to make hypotheses. Teachers stimulate children's thinking skills when they ask Socratic questions:

- "How could you keep new shoes clean if you were walking on the grass and you saw that the grass was all muddy and wet and squishy with rain puddles'?"
- "How could the little puppy find his friend who is hiding in the big bushes in the garden?"
- "What could Maya do to make her friend Edu feel better after Edu tripped on a wastebasket and fell hard on the floor?"
- "In this picture, what do you suppose made that boy's hat fly off his head and go rolling down the street?"

○ The caregiver listens to children who are vocalizing, talking, or questioning and then responds with turn-taking talk to encourage child conversations.

- The caregiver adjusts her voice and language structure, tone, and pitch appropriately for each child across a variety of classroom situations and activities.
- The caregiver initiates conversations in informal situations involving daily care routines throughout the day.
- The caregiver responds to child comments and questions.
- The caregiver uses positive, reassuring words that help children learn correct labels, without criticizing their responses that may not be correct initially.
- The caregiver gives children opportunities to express themselves when they work at a creative activity by asking them about their work.
- The caregiver gives children new words when they indicate a readiness to accommodate a new word into their vocabulary.
- The caregiver uses open-ended questions to encourage thinking and more complex talk.

The Caregiver Recognizes and Takes Advantage of Teachable Moments

Each naturally occurring opportunity that a teacher notices and takes advantage of is called a *teachable moment*. Picking up on teachable moments throughout the day can enhance the learning career of each child. When an adult focuses on a situation directly involving the child, this makes it possible to reinforce a desired behavior, to extend understanding of a concept, to help a child make a connection between an emotion and an action, to

understand the point of view of another, or to provide a new vocabulary word.

In the parking lot outside the tall fence of the child care center, a huge delivery truck pulls up. Children leave their swings and sand play to run to the fence and gaze at the gigantic truck. Taking advantage of this teachable moment, the caregiver asks the children what they think the truck might be carrying. Some of the preschoolers can make out the letters for bananas painted on the side. This suggests that the truck carries food supplies. The children discuss with animation what other foods the truck might be carrying and how brave the driver is to drive such an *enormous* (a word that their teacher provides!) truck.

The beauty of the field of early childhood is that adults have so many opportunities during ordinary activities to capitalize on the teachable moment. There are times when the preplanned activities of the classroom are laid aside to attend to a new situation: A torrential downpour outside fascinates the children. Hearing the thunder roar, they interrupt a planned activity and rush to peer through the windows and ask questions about winds lashing the tree branches, dark grey clouds, lightning and thunder, and the pouring rain. They see people walking bent over against

strong winds and struggling with umbrellas turned inside out. The teacher can talk with them about the sounds they hear, where rain comes from, what causes thunder to be so loud—so many learning opportunities!

On coming into the room one morning, the teacher and children hear strange sounds. A little black cricket has somehow gotten into the room. Teacher and children search the room and, by listening carefully, locate the tiny cricket in a corner of the room. They hold him gently and listen to his calls. They talk about what a cricket needs and then decide to carry him safely outdoors to the grass where he can find food and friends. Teachers take advantage of such special times and circumstances to enrich the world of children's experience and deepen their knowledge.

- The caregiver notices teachable moments and uses them to promote awareness and new understandings.
- The caregiver is able to put a scheduled curricular plan on hold to concentrate on a meaningful experience that might arise or that a child might introduce.

The Caregiver Is Sensitive to the Rhythms and Pacing of Days and Activities

There are varied rhythms to the days children spend in care. Sometimes children are excited, running around shouting outdoors with glee and riding trikes vigorously. Sometimes, all absorbed, they sit in a corner and examine each pinecone or slice of agate on a nature table with small, handheld magnifying glasses. Children may gallop with energy outdoors, but some seem to wilt by the end of the day. They suck a thumb more vigorously and anxiously. They often need a caregiver to caress them and speak in soothing, low, reassuring tones. Younger children may climb up on a teacher's lap and just cuddle quietly.

Transitions can be frustrating for young children. They need lots of notice that an activity is ending. They often need time to wind down from boisterous activity to a quieter exploration. Teachers need to give enough clear notice for a change—for example, that soon it will be time to put away toys and wash up for lunch. Play or sing a special tune or flick the room lights as clear signals that an activity transition will occur. Clear signals, such as chants, a few familiar piano chords, or special words, help ease the transition from one activity in which children are hard at play to another activity.

Ends of days when clean-up times are required are sometimes difficult. A caregiver who notices how tired children are late in the day may well pitch in to help put the blocks away and stack the puzzle sets. Tired children learn helpfulness and kindness as an adult works alongside them when a task seems too complicated or lengthy. A sensitive caregiver will consider the time of day and the individual child's temperament in setting reasonable expectations, such as at meal times when adult requests for neatness might be too hard for a sleepy child to comply with.

○ The caregiver balances opportunities during the day for quiet, more peaceful times and noisy, more boisterous times.
○ The caregiver offers optimal balances allowing for small- and large-muscle skill development.
○ The caregiver is sensitive to each child's developmental level and level of tiredness during activities.

○ The caregiver gives children appropriate notice and encourages peaceful transitions.

The Caregiver Promotes Children's Mental Health

What is mental health? Positive signs are when a person can experience loss, rejection, or discouragements in life and manage to cope well with these troubles, living comfortably with a positive sense of self and of others. The psychoanalyst Margaret Mahler has asserted that a child learns, with the support of loving adults, how to master feelings of anxiety when separated from the safe anchor of the caregiver. Before she is a year old, a baby gradually learns to feel pleasure in exploring the environment. Setting off to investigate toys on a shelf across the room, the baby may not even look back to check that the caregiver is still there. Innumerable small, intimate acts of kindness and reassurance have inspired bravery and support these early explorations. The securely attached baby feels sure that the adult remains always available. In case of a tumble or a sudden feeling of panic about being on her own, the baby is deeply confident that she can hurry back to her caregiver for some snuggling and reassurance. Wise caregivers help babies manage this separation-individuation process without undue anxiety. Babies dance emotionally between wanting to be molded on the body of the special caregiver and wanting to move and explore. Constancy helps the growing child to manage disappointments, to get up and try again.

When caregivers orchestrate this separation-individuation process with relaxed and skillful attentiveness during the early years, they are ensuring a child's mental health for years to come. With easy yet alert attention to individual differences in children's readiness for more mature behaviors, and with willingness to support children as they work toward attaining an inner balance between needing nurturance and enjoying self-actualized explorations and learning, caregivers promote mental health. They ensure sturdiness in emotional growth rather than vulnerability to feelings of intense loneliness, anxiety, or deep anger toward others.

Mental health problems can begin quite early in childhood. Twenty-one percent of children nine to seventeen years of age have a diagnosable mental health disorder (*Post-Standard*, 2012). Teachers and caregivers play a valuable role in preventing later mental health problems and promoting positive mental health. They validate children's feelings while teaching the difference between owning one's feelings and realizing that some actions are acceptable and some are not. All persons have strong feelings from time to time—some happy, some upsetting, some reasonable, some not. We may not hurt another person by acting on negative, angry, or resentful feelings. But, children do need adults to acknowledge the reality of their emotions and help them identify their emotions accurately. They need help in developing empathy to interpret others' feelings more accurately, too.

> Jimmy bopped Harry hard with a block when Harry moved close to him to watch him building a tower. Harry was curious. Jimmy felt mad—he believed that Harry might topple his tower! The teacher remarked, "Oh, Jimmy, you must be tired." But, Jimmy was not tired. He was defending his space and felt as if Harry might threaten his building project.

Crazymaking is a term that signifies that an adult is not giving clear information to a child about the difference between very strong, difficult feelings and carrying out actions that are inappropriate. Crazymaking occurs when a teacher either does not accept a child's right to have his own feelings or the teacher denies the reality or reasonableness of the child's own feelings and understandings of a situation. This also occurs when an adult combines praise and criticism in the same remark to the child; for example: "That's a nice picture, Joey, but you could draw much better than that if you tried harder."

Some other examples of crazymaking communication:

CHILD: Teacher, Sarah is sad. *(Sarah's grandfather died last week.)*

TEACHER: She'll be okay. How about doing some block building now?

CHILD: Teacher, I found a worm!

TEACHER: Ugh! Put that slimy thing down. It's time for lunch right now.

TEACHER: How many of you want to hear this CD about kangaroos?

KAREN, TAYSHAWN, and MIMI: No. Not me.

TEACHER: Well, here we go. I'll just put it on, and I'm sure that you will all enjoy this!

Annie bops Mark on the head.

TEACHER: We don't hit in the day-care center! *(Although, Annie just did hit!)*

Darren scribbles with a magic marker, looks at his paper happily, and then, satisfied, turns and gives the materials to his teacher.

TEACHER: Well, I guess that you didn't like that very much. You hardly spent any time on it.

Caregivers who promote good mental health give clear, supportive feedback that a child's feelings and perception of the world are as legitimate as anyone else's.

The teacher must provide a few simple classroom rules, such as no hurting others and no messing with other children's work, but the teacher can discuss the reasons for the rules with the children. Children depend on their special adults to help clarify and reaffirm their experiences with the world. Then, children gradually come to understand behavioral boundaries for themselves and for others. They learn to consider the causes and consequences of behaviors. As one preschooler murmured sadly after his teacher reminded him of the no-hitting rule: "And no kicking, either."

A child needs unconditional love and acceptance from special adults. It is challenging to build a loving relationship with a child and at the same time clarify strong negative, frightened, or angry feelings. One positive step to build good mental health is to acknowledge a child's right to her feelings while firmly discouraging inappropriate or hurtful actions. Promoting caring and empathy actively promotes prosocial relationships with others. Caregivers need to talk about feelings with children—their own and others'—to nurture empathy.

Using an accusatory *you* statement, such as, "Why did you knock all the toys off the table?" or asking, "Why did you hit Johnny?" often results in children feeling and acting defensive. Accusations may even impel a child to deny indignantly that she was responsible for a disapproved action. Then, the child might, in turn, make accusations against a peer: "He started it!" Let a child know feelings are legitimate. They are her feelings. When a child is angry, an adult can let her know that she can feel mad. But, the caregiver must communicate clearly the difference between accepting feelings and not allowing hurtful behaviors such as hitting, biting, cursing, or kicking others.

> Larry, you are feeling very mad. Jana knocked down your building that you have been working so hard on building. You can tell her so, but I cannot let you hit her, and I will not let others hit you if they are feeling angry. I need to keep everyone in our room safe! You can let her know just how you feel. You can tell her that you are feeling angry with her because she knocked down your tower. I will help you by reminding her clearly about our rules for respecting each other's work in our group. You can use your words to tell her, "I worked hard to build my tower! I need to keep on working on my building!"

A teacher has to help children see how they can heal a difficulty or a hurt. They can learn that they can summon the determination to rebuild a knocked-down block tower.

One powerful adult tool is to listen reflectively to children. When a child feels an adult is genuinely interested and paying attention to her feelings, this invests the child with a deep feeling of self-esteem. The adult confirms her truly cherishing feelings for the child. Reminiscing about her famous father, Marlo Thomas affirmed, "My dad wasn't perfect, but he had the laserlike ability to shut out the noisy world around him and listen to my sister and brother and me. To our worries. Our thoughts. Our feelings. I know that my confidence comes from having been truly heard as a child."

It helps when teachers state what they *do* want, not what they do not want. Children do not hear the *don't* in "Don't run." They may even run faster! It helps when teachers analyze situations and problems, and it helps when teachers specify clear behavioral limits and consequences for off-limits behavior.

Craig was intently building with blocks. Miss G had admired and urged him on and had praised each step. Another caregiver, Miss B came over and said, "Time to go to the gym." Craig pouted. He would not respond and would not go. Miss B picked him up in her arms, but he averted his face. "I wonder why he looks so mad and doesn't want to go," Miss B remarked cheerfully to Miss G.

"I think he wanted you to notice his tall tower and tell him it will be there after gym time," Miss G answered quietly.

"Oh, Craig, that's terrific," sang out Miss B, nodding her head vaguely in the tower's direction and walking off with a still-scowling Craig in her arms.

Craig needed to feel convinced that his teacher really understood how important his tower was for him. A teacher has to think of words and reassuring tones that convey definitively to the child that she does understand the worries and fears that might have caused a child's disobedience or defiance. Understanding what motivates a negative child behavior gives a powerful boost to being able to figure out how to meet the child's main worry or angry feeling. When a child's feelings are validated, he is much more likely to listen to a teacher's explanation of classroom rules or group needs. The child needs to feel that his teacher understands and cares about his feelings. A young child certainly cannot think intellectually in such terms, but the child will feel that his teacher hears and validates his fears, wishes, and need for reassurance in practical ways.

Craig needed an adult to reassure him that his building would be safe and that he would not find his building knocked down when he came back from the gym. He wanted the teacher to validate his concerns and to reassure him that she would protect his project and his work.

Caregivers who sharpen their noticing skills, particularly to assess emotional needs and states, will be more likely to read a child's signals of distress accurately. Reading body language well gives a boost to a caregiver's ability to promote good mental health. Watch for body-language signs. Does the child frown deeply? chew on a piece of hair or clothing? stiffen and draw away when the teacher attempts a hug? grind teeth? glare? clench fists? repeat a certain gesture over and over for reassurance? Watching for bodily signs of defensiveness, worry, and anger, an adult can figure out why a child is misbehaving or uncooperative. Then, the adult can make an effective plan for reasoning with, soothing, explaining, or comforting a child.

Young children can feel powerless. They may not yet have control over bladder and bowels. Some have troubles articulating words clearly. Some have not yet learned rules about not snatching toys from others. They have lots of learning to do to be able to share toys, plans for play, and play experiences together. Some are still surprised to hear a peer cry if they bite or pull hair or push a peer down. Teaching empathy is an important curricular goal for teachers of young children!

- **Use appreciation words, and model appreciation.** As Miss Cindy puts a shirt on Toby, she notices that he held up one arm. "Thank you, Toby. That is such a big help. You really helped me dress you more easily when you put up your arm. Thank you!"

- **Validate and confirm small acts of kindness.** "Tamar, you are holding on to that piece so patiently while Donna is trying to work the puzzle. You are waiting to hand that piece to Donna when she is ready to put it in the puzzle. You are being a good helper and friend with Donna."

"Thank you, Julie, for moving over so Jerrod could sit on the bench next to you and color a picture, too."

"Lilian, thank you for letting Chloe add pieces to the train track. Now you are both going to make an even longer track together."

"Gianni, thanks for finding Walt's teddy that fell out of his wagon. You brought it back to him. That was really kind of you. You know how to be a good friend!"

■ **Use the words *gently* and *carefully* over and over, and model those concepts with your own gestures.**

"Lisa, I know you want to rock Angie in the rocking chair, but she looks scared. Let's rock gently. See, if we rock gently, then Angie really likes when you rock the chair gently." As you say these words, put your hands over Lisa's hands so that she feels how gentle rocking is done.

■ **When a child has hurt another child, show the child how to help with making things better for the hurt child.**

"Oh, Jerry, when you pushed Tracy down, he fell and got hurt. Look, he is crying! We need to help him up. We need to get a warm, wet washcloth so we can soothe his arm where it looks red and feels bad. Come and help me get that washcloth ready."

■ **When you see an act of kindness, empathy, or helpfulness, say what you are seeing.** Children catch on and then often become more alert themselves to kind actions by peers (Honig and Pollack, 1990).

"Thank you for picking up Tina's cracker that fell from her high chair, Terry. She was crying and upset. That was so kind of you to give her cracker back to her."

"Donny, I see that you and Natalie are working together to build your fort. You make such a good team building together."

■ **Use bodily reassurance to teach nurturance when a child feels upset.** When sixteen-month-old Tyson started acting crabby after several weeks in child care, Mr. Aaron realized that perhaps Tyson was finally realizing that his mom was not there. So Mr. Aaron spent more time just carrying and cuddling Tyson that day. He realized that loving snuggles soothe more than words when a child suddenly becomes more aware of a parent's absence.

Consider that young children in other-than-parent care cannot be and have not been consulted about their placement with other adults. Some children are leisurely and dawdle a lot, yet they are rushed in the mornings, since parents need to get to jobs on time. Thus, children feel a lack of choice to decide for themselves in many areas of their lives, where parents must make decisions for their care and safety. Teachers empower children by offering small, appropriate choices whenever possible.

> After lunch, Linchi had a hard time falling asleep at nap time. His teachers felt frustrated that they could not have a quiet lunch time for themselves. Miss T offered a simple choice: "Linchi, which would you rather do? Do you want to sleep with your head at this end of the cot or at the other end? Linchi looked carefully and decided. "Good choosing," affirmed Miss T, and then Linchi settled onto his cot for a peaceful nap.

A youngster feels really important when consulted about even a simple decision. "Do you want apple juice or orange juice?" can help a child feel empowered to make her own decision.

❍ The caregiver tunes in to and sincerely listens to each child's feelings of worry, sadness, or anger as well as excitement and joy.

❍ The caregiver suggests helpful ideas for how to cope with strong upset or negative feelings.

❍ The caregiver helps children to understand their own and other's feelings.

❍ The caregiver encourages autonomy and offers safe choices that allow for individual child preferences when possible.

❍ The caregiver provides positive affirmations of the goodness of each child.

The Caregiver Uses a Variety of Positive Discipline Techniques

The effective caregiver tries hard to see ahead and prevent problems. Building inner controls among young children takes time, trust, and patience. Having a large supply and variety of positive discipline techniques serves a caregiver well in dealing with puzzling or difficult child behaviors. Creative structuring of learning episodes can minimize child frictions and fusses.

For example, if, at music time, a teacher dumps all the rhythm instruments in a heap in the center of a circle where the children were seated expectantly waiting, a melee is likely to ensue. The preschoolers will scramble over one another and knock into each other in their haste to reach a preferred instrument. The teacher may prevent conflict by offering each child a choice from the box and by having some duplicates of the more attractive instruments.

With infants and toddlers, creative prevention techniques are very handy for teachers to use, especially as toddlers enter the "terrible twos," where wills are strong and skills may be in short supply (Honig, 2005). Suppose a baby creeps toward another and tries to pull hair or push. Rather than fuss and give long explanations, a teacher of very young children will often scoop up that child and redirect her attention in an enthusiastic way to an interesting and safe activity.

Keeping promises consistently as a staff policy is a good technique for building up children's faith that they will get their turn, that there will be enough cookies to go around, that they will get their needs met. It is best to keep promises to a minimum. If a teacher promises that the children will go outside and play on the new slide after nap time, and then a rainstorm comes up, that promise will not be kept. Promises should reassure a child that you will be there to listen to a problem, to kiss a boo-boo, to retrieve a toy that has rolled far out of reach under a piece of furniture. A child who feels uncertain about trusting adult promises may need a bit more consideration.

> Ms. Sims had prepared a sensory box with a black cloth covering the box front. Inside the box were a hairbrush, some keys on a chain, a comb, and a toy banana. The children sat in chairs waiting for their turn to feel what was inside the box, then pick up the matching item on the table. Ms. Sims had promised each child a turn. Barry sat in the last chair in the row. He kept rocking his chair back and forth impatiently. Finally, he rocked the chair so hard it fell and also knocked down the chair of the child sitting next to him.

> Later, seeing the videotape of this lesson, Ms. Sims realized that Barry had little experience at home with promises being kept. He found waiting very difficult. Ms. Sims realized that Barry should have been given a turn earlier in the game.

Use specific praise with children. Some folks give lavish but very vague praise, such as, "Good job!" This catch-all phrase will not help children to understand exactly what is expected or admired. Specific praise, on the other hand, does help children understand. Praising specific positive behaviors increases the chance that children will behave more appropriately. Using children's names lovingly and often alerts them to listen more closely. Teachers promote cooperation when they provide clear descriptions of behaviors they admire and want to acknowledge and confirm:

Jody, you moved over so nicely to give Lou a chance to sit at the table with you. And then, you moved the crayon box so it was close to where both of you could reach crayons to color. Thank you for being such a kind friend to Lou.

Terry, you really helped find all the blue blocks scattered around on the floor. You put them away on the shelf where the blue blocks go. That was a big help! We can get our cleanup done so much more quickly now because of your help. We will have more time for singing together!

Melissa, Gerry really wanted you to give his teddy bear a ride in your wagon, but he did not ask you. I am so glad you stopped and offered his teddy a ride when you noticed how interested he was in your wagon and how he was holding out his teddy bear toward you. That was so friendly and helpful of you.

Betsy, you felt frustrated and mad when Fred pulled that hunk of clay closer to his end of the table where you are both making clay art. I am glad you called really loudly for me to come over, so I could remind Fred of our rule that the clay stays in the middle of the table where you can both reach it. That was good thinking!

Sometimes a teacher needs to enter into role plays to guide and entice a child into cooperative behaviors. Pretend grocery shopping and cooking is a game that can help when a child needs a boost in learning harmonious social pretend play. For example, a teacher might say, "Oh, Judy, I forgot to buy pancake mix. I promised we would make pancakes for our lunch party today and then invite other kids to come join us. Let's decide what we need for making pancakes, and then you can go to the store to buy the ingredients." By setting up role plays that require cooperative gestures, the teacher can encourage a child to participate in interactive, cooperative role play.

○ The caregiver uses distraction and redirection techniques judiciously.
○ The caregiver uses dramatic role play to engage a child in more acceptable activities as an alternative to more troublesome ones.
○ The caregiver restates clearly and succinctly rules for nonacceptable behaviors: "No hitting or hurting"; "No throwing toys"; "No calling others hurtful names."
○ The caregiver keeps promises to a minimum and follows through on promises made.
○ The caregiver gives specific praise that encourages desirable behaviors.

The Caregiver Instills a Love of Books, Stories, Writing, and Reading

Children start writing by scribbling pretend grocery lists or lists of wishes for Santa. They slowly start to write real letters among the scribbles, as they learn first some letters of their own names and then other letters. Some learn *M* from a fast-food sign. Others learn *S* from a stop sign. Many children ask teachers to take down their stories, their dreams, and their letters to grandparents who live far away. They love to dictate their tales and have the teacher read back their very own stories.

The slow steady growth from scribbles to adding "real" letters among the scribbles and drawings to invented spelling is such an amazing process. Children try to write what they hear—for example: "hrs lv heer" for "horses live here." Teachers can smile with admiration as children struggle creatively to write using their unique invented spellings.

Children relish stories with rhymes and repeated cadences and phrases (Gilman, 1992). The popularity of TV commercials teaches us how captivated children are by commercial rhymes and rhythmic jingles they almost effortlessly memorize. In his review of Robert Munsch's article on storytelling as an interaction, Roger Neugebauer (2012) reports, "When reading stories to young children, one can replace the word cadences with actions." So, as Goldilocks walks toward the house of the three bears in the forest, she sees a door and says, "Aaaaaa, door!" Then, when she reaches the door, she says, "Thump, thump, thump." The children soon learn to chime in with echoed actions and words. Combinations of words and gestures they can chant over and over keep children riveted both on the tale and on the storyteller.

Quality caregivers read expressively to children every day. Sharing picture books and reading daily with young children increases their zest for book reading, language skills, and interest in stories. Daily reading with children is more likely to result in early school success (Jalongo, 2007). Sharing picture books and using dialogic talk—discussing pictures with the children and asking them for their ideas and experiences that might be like those of the storybook characters—enhances language skills. Grover Whitehurst et al. (1994) found that dialogic talk is particularly helpful for low-income children both at day care and at home. In her book *Boys and Girls:*

Superheroes in the Doll Corner, Vivian Paley relates that she encouraged children in her classroom to create and dictate stories to her and then asked them to choose peers to act out their stories that she had written down. How eagerly the children looked forward to their "plays" being produced!

○ The caregiver shares picture books and reads every day with children.

○ The caregiver reads with rich emotional tones and sensitivity to children's interests to awaken their passion for books.

○ The caregiver talks about pictures with the children and asks them for their ideas and experiences that might be like those of the storybook characters.

○ The caregiver provides workspaces for scribbling and drawing and provides opportunities for each child to dictate a story that can be acted out in class.

The Caregiver Shares an Adventurous Love of Learning

Children get excited if their teacher shares that she is also a learner. When they hear that their teacher has tried canoeing or kayaking, is learning to play the piano or guitar, took part in a running marathon over the weekend, or has joined a choral group in the community, children feel that their teacher, too, partakes of the great adventure of learning.

To help a caregiver be a continuing learner in the field of child development, the director needs to provide resources and materials and arrange for appropriate ongoing, in-service training as well as training opportunities in local or national venues. The art of helping children grow well and true to their highest potential demands of educators a consuming curiosity to keep on learning more about how best to optimize children's growth and development. Caregivers can borrow books and articles on file in the director's office, can benefit from watching a more experienced teacher role-model effectively with a child, can try out new ideas for activities with children, and can share ideas and support each other in optimizing learning experiences for the children.

○ The caregiver shares with the children an exciting learning adventure in her own life.
○ The caregiver reads child-development materials, attends early childhood education workshops, and shares new ideas and learning experiences with the children.

The Caregiver Has the Energy Required for Daily Child Care Work

Orchestrating the daily schedule and working with groups of young children, planning for their needs, and individualizing interactions to meet specific needs takes a great deal more energy than many other jobs. In this labor-intensive work, a caregiver may at one moment be on the floor playing with a child and the next helping to haul tricycles out of a shed in the yard. At another time a care provider may have to tug off six pairs of tight rubber rain boots or clean up an inadvertently overturned jar of poster paint.

An energetic, enthusiastic caregiver can share her energy with a child who is tuned out or turned off from learning. Enthusiasm is contagious, and children's curiosity and caring can spark to life with the influence of a teacher who is excited about learning.

○ The caregiver has the physical well-being to care for young children for a full work day.
○ The caregiver has the psychological and emotional energy to encourage curiosity and excitement about learning.

The Caregiver Provides a Positive Model of Empathy and Compassion

Young children learn by identifying with the special adults in their lives. A caregiver who has formed a trusting, loving relationship with a child can teach so much just by the way she behaves. Research by social-learning theorists has taught us just how powerful an emotional impact the adult model can have. Preschoolers who watched a brief filmed episode of a big bully stealing a little child's toys, weeks later were able to remember all the details and vividly re-enact the role of the bully in that scene when invited to do so (Bandura, Ross, and Ross, 1963). Children are wondrous (and sometimes disastrously comical) imitators of adult roles, qualities, and styles.

Children learn empathy and caring for others from having consistently experienced nurturing responses when they are worried, have a stubbed toe, or need reassurance. They learn compassion by seeing how adults treat children

compassionately, despite exasperation when a child, for example, overturns a bowl of cereal on her head in the middle of a meal. Adults who use *please* and *thank you* encourage children to use more socially appropriate words rather than blurting out, "Gimme that toy!"

As teachers model enthusiasm for learning and model empathy and compassion, kindness and helpfulness, positive discipline methods, and gracious social relations with other staff, children are likely to imitate their teachers.

Teachers who model empathic and nurturing actions can mention out loud when they notice kind actions among children. Some teachers keep a sunshine jar into which they put a note about a caring action they have just noted and mentioned aloud. After a while, children themselves learn to call out when they see a kind action, and then *they* remind the teacher to make a note to put in the sunshine jar.

If the world has meaning for the well-loved caregiver, then the world will have meaning for the child. If adults are purposeful and reflecting, if adults are kind and considerate, then children imitate the adults who cherish them. In turn, children learn how to be caring persons.

○ The caregiver provides a prosocial role model for empathy, kindness, patience, and courtesy with all persons.
○ The caregiver notices aloud when children exhibit empathy, kindness, patience, and courtesy.

The Caregiver Respects the Unique Temperament and Personhood of Each Child

Most children come into the world with one of three major temperament styles: feisty, flexible, or fearful (Honig, 1997b). Feisty children are triggery and intense. For highly active children, a teacher must provide safe ways to let off steam, such as a rocking horse in a corner of the room where an intense toddler can climb on by herself and vigorously rock back and forth. Some feisty children cannot tolerate frustration even at mild levels. They cry hard; yet, they may also laugh loudly when amused. They may be irritable and harder to soothe than a less intense child who has a more flexible temperament and who adapts more easily to change, whether in food, schedule, or care providers. Fearful children are apt to act shy and cautious about approaching anything new, even a happy and sociable activity such as riding on a low seesaw with another child. They need more caregiver help and reassurance in approaching and getting involved with new experiences. Cautious children need the caregiver to take them by the hand and stay with them for a while, before they can feel comfortable and settle into a new activity.

○ The caregiver is tuned in to each child's temperament style.
○ The caregiver is responsive to any sensory sensitivities a child may have.

The Caregiver Meets the Children's Sensuous Needs

Young children live in a world of sensory-motor experiences. Watch a child's intense, absorbed concentration as she plays with water in a tub with containers, toy eggbeaters, cups, and sieves. Her tongue thrusts out as she carefully tries to pour water from one cup to another. How young children love to mess about with fingerpaints, sand, sawdust, rice, playdough, soapy water, or mud! Watch the satisfying pleasure a child gets from splashing at bath time. On a hot summer day, children scream with glee as they race through a spray of cool water on the lawn outside their classroom. Cooking and eating experiences provide a fine opportunity for rolling dough or smelling the ripeness of a fragrant apple that the caregiver carefully peels and slices for all to taste.

Young children love to squish hands through wet mud or sand. They love to lick and taste yummy foods. *Mess* is not in a young child's vocabulary. Safe sensory enjoyment is essential to their daily dose of pleasure. Stamping in a puddle with boots on, splashing in a baby pool on a warm summer day, squashing crisp fall leaves underfoot, tasting snowflakes on the tongue with a face upturned to the snowy sky—all these provide sensory delights for little ones and can lead to group glee and gales of giggles.

When children are provided with outdoor nature experiences, they absorb their needed dose of what Richard Louv calls "N" vitamins (nature vitamins). Louv, co-founder of the Children and Nature Network, reports that memory performance and attention spans are enhanced as children get their "green exercise . . . their dose of vitamin N" (Louv,

2012).

Most children grin with enjoyment as they play with bubble solutions. Crawling babies try to catch the rainbow-hued bubbles on their hands and squeal happily. Yet, a caregiver also has to be aware that some children are overly sensitive to certain tastes, touches, and other sensory experiences. The teacher must consider a child's temperament and sensory needs. She should not force a child, for example, to mush with his fingers and explore cornstarch goop if he reacts very negatively to that sensation.

Self-stimulation is common when young children feel stressed. A preschooler may suck his thumb vigorously when overstimulated by new sights or situations or twirl pieces of her hair to soothe herself. A withdrawn toddler may sit quietly on the floor, rocking his body back and forth.

Sensory needs are strong. Young children lick and munch on food as if delighted as much with the texture and taste as well as with filling their bellies. When given a hunk of ripe banana, some babies are as likely to find as much pleasure in squishing the banana through their fingers as in biting off a bit to eat. While carrying a baby, a caregiver might be amused to see the little one lean down and lick the caregiver's arm. Children are sensuous creatures. Hold a baby up to a mirror, and she may lean forward to lick or stroke her own reflection as she vocalizes.

A teacher provides "E" vitamins (emotional vitamins) for a tired or worried child by snuggling the child for a story or a quiet time or by wrapping a comforting arm around the child. Caressing physical gestures also serve as sensuous experiences that nourish the child's positive sense of self while satisfying a child's needs for bodily contact comfort.

○ The caregiver peaceably accepts the sensuous personal nature of little ones.
○ The caregiver provides experiences with water play, clay, playdough, fingerpaint, and other sensory explorations.
○ The caregiver provides sensory experiences by serving foods attractively and by engaging children in sniffing and tasting experiences.
○ The caregiver plans for and provides outdoor nature experiences for the children.

The Caregiver Has High, Individualized Expectations for Each Child

Children come to a center with different levels of attention span and persistence, as well as varying ability levels. Some children have few social skills but may be adept at using a computer or solving a many-piece puzzle or may even be able to read a simple Dr. Seuss book. Some climb and swing with ease, while others appear fearful of climbing up even two steps. All children need to be challenged in unhurried, unpressured ways to become more competent.

A care provider should communicate positive acceptance and belief in each child's ability to grow in understanding and in skills. Teachers need to formulate individualized goals for each child, and strong expectations that their own creativity, caring, and intelligent curricular orchestration will truly encourage each child to blossom.

Some children in group care have delays in mobility or in language. Some children have challenges that peers may react to with fear, ridicule, or avoidance. All children need acceptance and friendship. A teacher needs well-honed observation skills and kind yet firm interventions to help children accept all their peers. It surely is a creative challenge for teachers to work with children with different bodily troubles, emotional troubles, or ability levels. It is not always easy to figure out what techniques and interactions will work best in each situation as teachers try hard to meet each individual child's needs (Honig, 1997a).

○ The caregiver makes a concerted effort to learn about each individual child's strengths and difficulties.

○ The caregiver supports each child's individual level of interest and ability.

○ The caregiver supports acceptance and a nurturing atmosphere in the classroom.

The Caregiver Acts to Make Families Feel Welcome in the Program

Dropping off a child in day care may be done in a hurried fashion as parents rush off to work. Days may end on a tired note at pick-up time. Finding ways to promote good parent-center cooperation for child development is a challenge for the caregiver.

A caregiver can find creative ways to communicate with busy families. She may safety pin a "Memo to Parent" to a child's coat. Small notes might say, "Helen mixed yellow and blue paint and made green today all by herself!" "Joey and his friend Billy built a spaceship out of blocks." "Danny is beginning to point to pictures in books and tell us the names of animals." The teacher suggests brief printed materials (Honig, 2000; 2004) and websites to assist family members who want to learn more about child development and optimal parenting.

Caregivers who approach families as a valued source of information about a child often ask parents to share their special knowledge about their child with staff (Honig, 1975). If a teacher is puzzled by a child's rare smiles, the teacher can ask the parent to share what family members have noticed that makes the child smile; an uncle who makes funny faces may be just the person who evokes wide grins. Families can offer information and insight about favorite games, foods, and playmates at family gatherings or in the neighborhood.

Parents feel accepted when we ask them about their child's favorite toy, lovey, food, or game. When there is a genuine culture difference between the center or caregiver and some families' beliefs, try to find a way to compromise. For example, in some cultures, a parent will continue to feed a toddler long after a child that age is easily able to feed himself. Talk with the parent about how to compromise, perhaps by letting the child feed himself on some days and by letting the parent come in at lunch time and feed him on other days.

Sometimes a teacher simply has to quietly restate the rules of the center. In one center I was visiting, I heard a scream and saw that a parent had taken out a hairbrush and was smacking a child. The director quickly and quietly moved close and, in a low, firm voice, restated the center rules that no child is ever to be hit in child care. She invited that parent in for a talk about different ways to teach a child to listen and obey. Some folks come from families where "scold and hit" are major methods of discipline. Other parents assume that a young child's abilities to listen and obey are far more advanced than that child can yet manage. That is why sharing knowledge about ages and stages and developmental milestone norms needs to be an integral part of parent-staff get-togethers.

When families speak another language, caregivers often worry about how to include a young child who is learning English. Toy telephone games can help as children giggle an unintelligible message into the toy telephone to each other from across the room. Use chants and pictures, and try group sharing games. Choose simple themes, one at a time, and act them out. For example, sing out, "I have a foot." Encourage each child to wiggle a foot in the air while seated in a circle on the floor. Continue with other words such as the following:

- I have socks.
- I wear mittens on my hands.
- I brush my hair.
- I drink juice.
- I pull up my jacket zipper all by myself.
- I brush my teeth.
- I can wiggle my fingers.
- I can pat my tummy.

Encourage children who are learning English as a second language (ESL) to say the words in their home languages. During such circle times, ESL children can learn the English words, and English-speaking children can learn some words in other languages.

Another way to enhance language learning is through ball-throwing games. As children play catch with a large, soft ball, they can practice saying, "Throw it to me," "Over here," "I get the ball next," "My turn," or "I catch the ball now" in English and other languages. As one child told his dad who had been posted to a Spanish-speaking country, "I just say *aqui*, and the ball comes to me, Dad!" He was not yet aware that *aqui* means "here" in Spanish but had learned to use that word to participate in a ball game with peers.

It is particularly lovely when caregivers learn some affectionate and loving words in other languages, such as *cara* ("dear one" in Italian), *mi amor* ("my love" in Spanish), *chéri* ("darling" in French), or *habibi* ("my darling" in Arabic). Words that express admiration are important, too. When a teacher learns some admiration words in another language, children who are learning English can feel included and appreciated. Try *muy hermosa* ("very beautiful" in Spanish), *bello* or *bella* ("lovely" in Italian), or *yasashi* ("gentle" in Japanese). Talk with families to learn appropriate words to use in their home languages.

Learning some polite words from another language also can help children who are learning English feel more comfortable. For example, *Ta shi hao de* ("It is okay" in Mandarin) may be comforting words to a little fellow who has just spilled some juice or has torn a collage paper by accident.

Singing simple songs in other languages is fun for all children. Many toddlers garble the words but belt out "Frére Jacques" with enthusiasm. Invite parents who are willing to help teach the group some easy children's songs in their home language to visit your classroom. The more you express appreciation at their participation, the more willing parents will be to share aspects of their home cultures and the more comfortable they will feel with staff.

Comfort and joy with familiar songs extends to children who do speak English but come from distinct culture groups. I once sang all the stanzas to "Hush, Little Baby," and at the end of the song, an African-American little boy sat up on his cot and joyfully called out, "My mama sing that! My mama sing that to me!"

Immersion in a new language has been found to be the fastest way for children to learn that language. Yet, immersion in English has to go hand in hand with respect for and genuine enjoyment of learning words from the child's home culture, too. When possible, provide picture books in the home languages for the children to choose and browse through on their own. Children who are learning English will feel comforted as they turn the pages of picture books that show children who look like them and where each page has familiar cultural symbols or scenes.

A quality caregiver listens to a parent nonjudgmentally, even if the caregiver does not feel that some of the parent's concerns are ones that a teacher can or should deal with. The teacher above all tries to convey admiration for the parent who is trying so hard to carry out two important jobs: work and parenting. The teacher tries to convey how special the child is and how wonderful it is to be a helping partner with the parent so that this child will thrive and grow happily and well.

Center staff can convey their genuine caring for families by holding supper meetings where children show off their drawings and sing songs. They can invite parents in to share experiences and expertise such as crafts, stories, music, dances, or sports skills. Center teachers can ask parents for help on weekends if the facility needs to have a new slide set up on the playground. Some parents will enjoy making friends with other families as they work together to make the environment safe and pleasurable for the children. Children watch the ways in which their families and their teachers get along and learn to feel comfortable and secure because they see that these relationships are warm and accepting.

○ The caregiver finds ways to relate to parents so that children notice the teacher's caring and supportive communications with family members at drop-off and pick-up times.
○ The caregiver is comfortable interacting with children and families who come from different cultural backgrounds and may have limited English-speaking ability.
○ The caregiver offers copies of short articles or other resources for parents who have lots of childrearing questions and would like to learn more about child development.

The Caregiver Integrates the Day-Care Experience for Children

A caregiver who brings thoughtful intelligence and consideration to the job will manage to integrate the totality of the day-care experience for young children. Integration should occur along several dimensions:

- **Cognitive, language, and problem-solving activities:** Integrate these activities comfortably into the daily routines (Lally and Honig, 1977). The challenge lies in how feeding times, nap times, toileting times, shepherding times, and clean-up times can become enriching experiences as well as necessary routines! Every ordinary experience has the potential to help children feel not only safe and cherished, but also can provide a special learning experience. Sensitive planning, awareness, and communication skills are required.

  An ordinary activity, such as walking back into the classroom after boisterous and vigorous outdoor play, offers an opportunity for learning. Children can learn to switch gears and walk quietly using lower voice tones. Changing activity locale lets children practice social skills to adapt to different requirements of outdoor and indoor spaces.

- **Humor:** A little humor adds a touch of a laid-back quality to the overall child care experience. The teacher who occasionally makes a joke or a gentle humorous comment with preschoolers and enjoys occasional giggles and laughter with children creates a more harmonious climate of care. A toddler jokes by thrusting her foot into an empty tennis-ball container then grins and says, "Shoe!" Young children love the format of knock-knock jokes even when they do not get the point of the joke.

- **Social and emotional supports:** The close meshing of cognitive enrichment with social-emotional supports in an atmosphere where loving and learning are intertwined helps children flourish.

The integration of experiences can be promoted if toys and activities are seen as actively supporting a variety of curricular goals: Play with a graduated ring-stack toy teaches spatial relations to young infants and also gives a boost to eye-hand coordination skills. Teachers can use the rings to label colors and the circle shapes. For preschoolers, a tall ring-stack set may appeal as a challenging seriation task; the rings must be placed in order from widest to narrowest for all to fit in sequence on the pole.

Setting out foods for snacks and meals meets not only children's nutrition needs but also can serve to teach numbers, shapes, tastes, colors, textures, ethnic specialties, and humanly satisfying sociable patterns. At meal times, children can improve wrist-control skills, learn food names, talk about family and culture, discuss foods they enjoy, and learn to use polite words, as well as feel proud that they are capable and can indeed scoop some food all by themselves from a serving bowl.

○ The caregiver uses each daily routine as a potential opportunity to enhance several goals to enrich children's development and maximize early learning.
○ The caregiver uses a light touch and a bit of simple humor with the children.

The Experienced Caregiver Is a Role Model for Aides, Volunteers, or Student Interns

The last checklist item relates to the attributes of seasoned caregivers and teachers who are already highly qualified in their work. After a caregiver has been in her position for a while, a director may wisely seek to use the teacher's professional skills for assistance in training or mentoring. Experienced teachers of young children often have the

responsibility to help their aides, volunteers, and teachers-in-training develop effective skills. Sharing ideas and experiences, providing positive feedback, and modeling successful techniques are some ways teachers can work with aides, volunteers, and students interested in studying early childhood.

○ The seasoned teacher who is designated to help aides, volunteers, and student interns makes the newcomers feel welcome, receiving them warmly, explaining the daily schedule and routines, and introducing them to co-workers, parents, and children.

○ The supervising teacher creates an environment where volunteers, aides, and less experienced teachers feel comfortable to observe and to participate in planning whenever appropriate.

○ The supervising teacher speaks with those supervised to provide explanations, to comment positively on successful interactions, and to ask Socratic questions to help them consider and reflect on their own efforts.

○ The more experienced teacher takes advantage of teachable moments to suggest a variety of activities and interactions that reflect effective techniques and reinforce early childhood principles.

USING THE CARE QUALITY CHECKLIST

The care quality checklist consists of twenty-four questions. Underneath each of the first twenty-three questions are descriptions of what caregivers are doing and how they are interacting with each child with respect to the content of that question. The checklist makes it possible to rate and reveal how well caregivers are fulfilling the "recipe" for high-quality care that includes the priceless interpersonal ingredients that help young children thrive in other-than-parent care.

For each interaction or behavior, explanations and descriptions of positive adult behaviors and interactions help checklist users understand why this is an important ingredient in providing quality child care. Descriptions and explanations of behaviors refresh an observer's understanding of the domain components of each item and increase chances for accurate ratings. These reflections make it more likely for raters to feel confident in their rating decisions. The observer can watch a caregiver's interactions and then determine the rating that best represents the quality of care observed.

The four-point scale specified beneath each numbered checklist question allows an observer to rate the degree to which a care provider is carrying out each behavior. The ratings range from "practically never" to "practically all of the time." Subcategories under several of the items allow for a fine-grained rating of how much or how little certain specific behaviors have been observed.

When to Observe

Checklist users will need to be sensitive in deciding when to observe. For example, observing a caregiver's interactions with the children right after a fire drill has caused commotion would not give a fair, accurate understanding of the day-to-day nurturing care that a teacher provides. Similarly, if a director is aware that a child has spent a stressful weekend witnessing family violence or marital anger, he should consider that the child may behave differently than is typical, in terms of internalizing behaviors or aggressive behaviors (Davies, Cicchetti, and Martin, 2012). A director is likely to get a more valid picture of the child-caregiver relationship if observations are carried out at different times of day and on different days during the week.

The rater may observe interactions with all of the children in the group, or the rater may choose to focus on teacher interactions with a particular child who has special needs or has presented particular issues such as frequent biting or extreme shyness with peers. The use of the checklist depends on a particular "need to know" for a given user. The director may use all of the items on the checklist or only those that address a particular area of interaction.

It is important to remember, in fairness to the care providers, that judgments should only be made about the quality of care after many careful observations, at different times of the day and on different days of the week. Children's behaviors and teacher responses do vary when children are tired, hungry, or have spent long hours in child care.

How to Examine the Information

When several observations have been carried out over a sufficient period of time, the director can make an overall cumulative judgment of the degree to which the caregiver is fulfilling each interaction domain on the checklist. In reviewing the information with the teacher, the director or mentor can discuss areas where the teacher is performing well and areas where more development or training may be needed.

A Tool for Directors

Directors have many demands on their time—they do not have hours to spend in classrooms observing a new teacher.

The care quality checklist can be a helpful information-gathering tool for busy directors. They can use it whenever they can find the time to begin filling out what will be essentially a portrait of a caregiver's ways of being and behaving with each child in the group.

Center directors can find the checklist particularly useful in making hiring decisions and in evaluating new teachers. Often, directors feel frustrated when needing to hire new teachers—sometimes they are constrained because salaries are lower than they rightfully should be for this specialized, essential work of nurturing young children. Sometimes a particular applicant may not have had opportunities for designated training that the director wishes an applicant had. Yet, the director may find the potential caregiver to be a warm, loving, enthusiastic person who has already shown devotion to children through life experiences, such as extensive provision of informal child care, rather than through more formal coursework and training. The director may well want to give such a candidate an opportunity to show child care sensitivities and skills in the classroom before making a definitive hiring decision.

The checklist is particularly useful in deciding whether or not to offer a permanent job to a person in a temporary position. A try-out period for a new provider is a helpful idea: Before making a definite hiring decision, directors can offer an aspiring caregiver a chance to work with a more experienced teacher in the classroom for several weeks or months. This gives the director a chance to observe and determine if the new recruit is a good fit to work with other classroom teachers, to work with a particular age group, to learn the ways of this particular facility, and to handle flexibly all the varied tasks that are involved in quality child care.

The checklist provides questions about two dozen attributes that signal responsive, quality caregiving. A director can focus on each question and its subitems and then rate the degree to which the new teacher exhibits interactions representing different ways of responding in that domain. Each rating provides an index of how well the new or potential employee is fulfilling each interpersonal domain. When repeated over a try-out period, the checklist gives the director information on the teacher's progress over time. A decision for permanent hiring is easier if the director's ratings show that the new care provider is learning and is fulfilling many of the positive tasks and attributes listed in the checklist.

If a director is overburdened and busy fulfilling other responsibilities at the facility, she may choose to enlist the help of students of child development from nearby colleges. By learning to use the checklist, student interns who are knowledgeable about child development research and theory may be able to provide daily support for the director's decision making. Of course, any permanent hiring decisions would be based on more than one set of observations. Observer ratings by an outside volunteer may prove helpful as an additional source of information in supporting a director's decisions. Extra eyes and ears can be particularly useful to a director in assessing the quality of the relationships of teachers with young children.

A Tool for Mentor Teachers

Experienced teachers are often asked to mentor less experienced caregivers. The care quality checklist can help with this process. When used as a teaching tool, the checklist offers concrete feedback that a mentor can use to help a caregiver understand how to interact with young children. Nurturing, supportive, rich relationships develop over time, and a mentor can help an inexperienced teacher learn ways to create a caring environment in which these relationships can flourish.

A Tool for Caregivers-in-Training

A caregiver or teacher can also use this checklist as a self-assessment guide to help navigate the weeks of pre-service training or early in-service teacher work. Using the feedback from the checklist, a teacher will gain more insights into effective and zestful ways of interacting with and facilitating young children's learning and emotional growth. The checklist can help teachers reflect continuously on their personal interactions and on ways to increase the sophistication, breadth, and in-depth relationships with the children they serve, as well as to increase their own joy in becoming the best possible teachers of young children!

A Tool for Agencies that Fund Child Care Facilities

Sometimes a community agency is responsible for funding and supervising several child care facilities. Agency personnel will want to use instruments that assess the quality of child care settings and materials. In addition, they may want to focus more specifically on the quality of the relationship of staff with the children for each center. The checklist offers this specific focus and can serve to support any agency decisions to offer further supports, such as staff training funds, to a particular center.

A Tool for Parents

Working parents need to choose caregivers they trust, so that the family members will have peace of mind, knowing that their children are safe, nurtured, and well cared for. Most community resource and referral agencies are excellent resources for providing names and locations of child care facilities. Usually, however, these agencies do not provide any indicators of quality. The checklist provides a practical tool for parents who are trying to choose the best fit for their child. Families who have chosen family or friends rather than a child care center as care providers may also want to use the checklist items to informally assess how well their child is being cared for. The specific tips and explanatory descriptions of behaviors provided with each checklist item heighten a parent's awareness of what to look for when observing a care provider's interactions with their child, whether in a child care center or in a family child care setting.

Some children adjust easily to child care; some children adapt more slowly. Many parents do not have time for lengthy or frequent visits to a facility to gauge the quality of care offered. Parents can use the checklist to observe interactions and situations after a child's initial adjustment period in a care facility. They can choose to observe only a few of the checklist categories at a time, taking advantage

of short observation periods to focus on specific aspects of caregiving that seem personally most important to them. Parents can sharpen their noticing skills and decide more clearly whether the interactions observed and the activities and care provided make this space a good fit for their child.

A Tool for Use in Parent Meetings

A director may choose to share with individual families the information she has gathered using the care quality checklist. The questions focus on areas that are often of concern to parents: will the teacher read to their child, assist with toilet learning or self-feeding skills, or hold her when she needs some extra reassurance? Parents of newborns often have other primary worries. After a baby is born, many families feel stressed in trying to find care they can trust, so that a new mother can return to employment. The checklist can help reassure parents that not only is the care center offering safe, healthy care for their child, but the center is also focusing on the quality of one-on-one care.

During parent-night gatherings, directors can discuss a few of the checklist questions and share how the caregivers are working to meet the one-on-one needs of each child. Teachers and parents can share ideas and partner on ways to nurture the children. Partnering with parents helps them feel deeply reassured that their children are receiving optimal care in this facility and are being specifically helped to grow as enthusiastic young learners.

With parents whose children have developmental challenges, a director may want to spend more time on the importance of only a few of the items, such as promotion of language or mental health. Many facilities for early care are moving toward inclusion of children with a variety of developmental difficulties. This increases the challenge for teachers to become adept at facilitating interactions for children with developmental challenges that sometimes make peer interactions problematic. Parents may focus, for example, on their hope that teachers will ensure that children who have rudimentary group-entry skills learn ways to join in peer-play scenarios. Caregivers can partner with parents to support the children in their growth and development.

THE CARE QUALITY CHECKLIST

Twenty-three of the questions are specifically focused on and important for decision making about the quality of care each child is experiencing. Explanations of the meaning and importance of each listed item is provided prior to the item listing. Under some of the main items, raters will find specific subcategories. Each reflects in more detail one of the checklist behaviors that indicate whether and how much a caregiver is exhibiting or addressing the behaviors and caregiver qualities. The twenty-fourth question refers to an experienced teacher's ability to mentor a classroom aide or volunteer.

Some of the questions may be more important for a teacher of older preschoolers or a teacher working with young infants. Some raters might decide to focus on questions where the responses are of greater interest with respect to a particular child or for a particular classroom. The last question focuses on how well an experienced caregiver has been able

to serve as a model for newer staff members. Some adults are superb caregivers with young children but may not feel comfortable supervising other adults. Other highly gifted teachers are more at ease and confident in assuming a mentoring role with a new teacher or classroom assistant.

1. Is the caregiver a nourisher?

A quality caregiver nourishes a child's fundamental feeling of being lovable, providing tuned-in companionship for each of the children. The nourishing caregiver shares joy and tenderness while providing deeply affirmative care.

A. Are the teacher's voice tones positive and genuinely caressing?
- ○ Practically never
- ○ Some of the time
- ○ Most of the time
- ○ Practically all of the time

B. Does the teacher frequently and generously provide lap and snuggling times?
- ○ Practically never
- ○ Some of the time
- ○ Most of the time
- ○ Practically all of the time

C. Does the adult get down on the floor with young children and play with them?
- ○ Practically never
- ○ Some of the time
- ○ Most of the time
- ○ Practically all of the time

D. Does the caregiver rub the backs of children at nap time and/or use a rocking chair to settle and soothe a fretful child?
- ○ Practically never
- ○ Some of the time
- ○ Most of the time
- ○ Practically all of the time

E. Does the teacher conscientiously attend to the children's safety, health, and physical well-being?
- ○ Practically never
- ○ Some of the time
- ○ Most of the time
- ○ Practically all of the time

2. Is the caregiver a good classroom arranger?

The quality caregiver arranges the classroom in ways that help the children clearly understand the purpose for each area. He provides a variety of materials for the children and offers open-ended and closed-ended opportunities for exploration. Children have opportunities for large- and small-muscle skill development and both boisterous and quiet play.

A. Does the caregiver provide opportunities for the children to use open-ended materials as well as closed-ended materials?
   - ○ Practically never
   - ○ Some of the time
   - ○ Most of the time
   - ○ Practically all of the time

B. Does the caregiver provide areas where children can safely play with water in tubs with different floatable and sinkable toys?
   - ○ Practically never
   - ○ Some of the time
   - ○ Most of the time
   - ○ Practically all of the time

C. Does the caregiver provide areas where children can play with dry materials, such as tubs with rice or sand, with different small toys hidden inside?
   - ○ Practically never
   - ○ Some of the time
   - ○ Most of the time
   - ○ Practically all of the time

D. Does the caregiver provide opportunities for vigorous movement and large-muscle activity?
   - ○ Practically never
   - ○ Some of the time
   - ○ Most of the time
   - ○ Practically all of the time

E. Does the caregiver provide areas, work centers, or tables where children can practice small-muscle skills with appropriate materials?
   - ○ Practically never
   - ○ Some of the time
   - ○ Most of the time
   - ○ Practically all of the time

F. Has the caregiver arranged a special space, safely within view of the teacher, for a child who needs time to cool off or to just settle down for a little while?
   - ○ Practically never
   - ○ Some of the time
   - ○ Most of the time
   - ○ Practically all of the time

G. Does the caregiver arrange room dividers and furniture so that attractive learning centers are available and marked so that children clearly can understand the uses for each area?

○ Practically never   ○ Most of the time

○ Some of the time   ○ Practically all of the time

3. Does the room where the children are cared for seem harmonious and aesthetically lovely to live in?

Aesthetics are important for young children. When adults provide peaceful, attractive, uncluttered settings, with interesting work areas and play areas, children enjoy learning while living in beautiful spaces.

A. Does the caregiver arrange environments for harmonious child interactions and for enhancing children's aesthetic sense of beauty and loveliness?

○ Practically never   ○ Most of the time

○ Some of the time   ○ Practically all of the time

B. Does the caregiver incorporate photos and other elements sent from children's homes to give a personal feel to the space?

○ Practically never   ○ Most of the time

○ Some of the time   ○ Practically all of the time

4. Is the caregiver a good observer?

A quality caregiver needs to watch body language, such as a scowling forehead, clenched fists, a tired shoulder droop, or eyes that avoid contact, and interpret child behaviors as accurately as possible. Teachers who observe carefully can devise ways to assist each child toward optimizing skills and abilities.

A. Does the caregiver observe children's body language and find caring ways to ease fears or encourage the frustrated child?

○ Practically never   ○ Most of the time

○ Some of the time   ○ Practically all of the time

B. Does the caregiver use creative and positive ways to help less socially adept children enter into playgroups with peers?

- ○ Practically never
- ○ Some of the time
- ○ Most of the time
- ○ Practically all of the time

C. Does the caregiver notice children's interests and preferences and capitalize on them by providing materials and props to facilitate complex play and pretend play experiences?

- ○ Practically never
- ○ Some of the time
- ○ Most of the time
- ○ Practically all of the time

5. Does the caregiver encourage competency at everyday personal tasks?

When children are invited to participate in daily routines, such as meal times, clean-up times, and planning times, they increase their competency skills and self-confidence.

A. At meal times, does the caregiver encourage children to help set out utensils, dishes, or napkins?

- ○ Practically never
- ○ Some of the time
- ○ Most of the time
- ○ Practically all of the time

B. Does the caregiver encourage the children to provide some help in clearing dishes and utensils after meals'?

- ○ Practically never
- ○ Some of the time
- ○ Most of the time
- ○ Practically all of the time

C. Does the caregiver encourage self-care with clothing and provide painting smocks that are easy to fasten and put on with minimal adult help?

- ○ Practically never
- ○ Some of the time
- ○ Most of the time
- ○ Practically all of the time

D. Does the caregiver offer specific praise and encouragement to children as they attempt everyday tasks?

- ○ Practically never
- ○ Some of the time
- ○ Most of the time
- ○ Practically all of the time

6. Does the caregiver boost thinking and reasoning skills?

Children are natural explorers and scientists. They ask questions, experiment, and investigate the world around them. Teachers can support this process by providing interesting opportunities for children to develop their thinking skills.

A. Does the caregiver help the child to reason, analyze, search actively for possible ways to sort items, and think of explanations and reasons for sorting in certain ways?

○ Practically never   ○ Most of the time

○ Some of the time   ○ Practically all of the time

B. Does the caregiver provide safe and supervised meal preparation opportunities for young children to learn transformations?

○ Practically never   ○ Most of the time

○ Some of the time   ○ Practically all of the time

C. Does the caregiver encourage the children to make shrewd, reasonable guesses: "What will happen if . . . ?"

○ Practically never   ○ Most of the time

○ Some of the time   ○ Practically all of the time

D. Does the caregiver provide opportunities for counting individual items and making numerical estimates to advance preschoolers' math skills?

○ Practically never   ○ Most of the time

○ Some of the time   ○ Practically all of the time

E. Does the caregiver teach concepts, such as opposites, in a positive way to further early learning?

○ Practically never   ○ Most of the time

○ Some of the time   ○ Practically all of the time

7. Is the caregiver a good "matchmaker"?

Using their perceptive noticing skills, caregivers tune in to each child's gifts and strengths. Teachers set reasonable learning goals, arrange materials, and offer experiences for discoveries that are neither too easy nor too difficult for each child. A quality caregiver matches experiences, suggestions, questions, and information to the level where each child can currently handle the ideas or actions involved.

A. Does the caregiver show awareness of and adjust for the level of difficulty of a task when working with each individual child?

○ Practically never   ○ Most of the time

○ Some of the time   ○ Practically all of the time

B. Does the caregiver prepare materials slightly varied in gradation of difficulty before beginning an activity to ensure that there will be an appropriate match for each child?

○ Practically never   ○ Most of the time

○ Some of the time   ○ Practically all of the time

8. Does the caregiver encourage creativity and the pleasures of pretend play?

Young children are attuned to and respond with joy to beauty. Nurturing a child's creativity, a caregiver increases a child's innate wonder in discovering aesthetic delights.

A. Does the caregiver provide rhythmic, musical, and chanting experiences?

○ Practically never   ○ Most of the time

○ Some of the time   ○ Practically all of the time

B. Does the caregiver encourage children to use their bodies expressively in dance, drama, costume, and movement to music?

○ Practically never   ○ Most of the time

○ Some of the time   ○ Practically all of the time

C. Does the caregiver set up a dress-up area with clothes that are appealing for boys and girls?

○ Practically never   ○ Most of the time

○ Some of the time   ○ Practically all of the time

D. Does the caregiver provide large cartons and/or other props to encourage pretend play?

○ Practically never   ○ Most of the time

○ Some of the time   ○ Practically all of the time

E. Does the caregiver actively promote children's role-play abilities and imaginative games?

- ○ Practically never
- ○ Some of the time
- ○ Most of the time
- ○ Practically all of the time

9. Does the caregiver provide positive contingent reinforcement (PCR)?

To boost children's positive behaviors toward goals, a caregiver needs to reward desired behaviors and, whenever possible, ignore more immature or inappropriate behaviors. Of course, adults cannot permit aggressive actions; they should use firm, calm ways to stop aggressive actions. PCR means that teachers give children prompt attention and positive feedback when the children are behaving appropriately or acting in ways that staff feel are developmentally desirable.

A. Does the caregiver provide positive, clear contingent reinforcement?

- ○ Practically never
- ○ Some of the time
- ○ Most of the time
- ○ Practically all of the time

B. Does the caregiver ignore, as much as possible, immature or inappropriate behaviors?

- ○ Practically never
- ○ Some of the time
- ○ Most of the time
- ○ Practically all of the time

10. Is the caregiver a language enlarger?

Quality caregivers extend conversations with young children, show genuine interest in their talk together, and give children time to find words to express their ideas and feelings (Honig, 2008). Creative language promoters use the varied occasions and circumstances of the child care environment and their own daily routines to enlarge children's language repertoires (Jalongo, 2007).

A. Does the caregiver listen to children who are vocalizing, talking, or questioning and then respond with turn-taking talk to encourage child conversations?

      ○ Practically never   ○ Most of the time

      ○ Some of the time   ○ Practically all of the time

B. Does the caregiver adjust her voice and language structure, tone, and pitch appropriately for each child across a variety of classroom situations and activities?

      ○ Practically never   ○ Most of the time

      ○ Some of the time   ○ Practically all of the time

C. Does the caregiver initiate conversations in informal situations involving daily care routines throughout the day?

      ○ Practically never   ○ Most of the time

      ○ Some of the time   ○ Practically all of the time

D. Does the caregiver respond to child comments and questions?

      ○ Practically never   ○ Most of the time

      ○ Some of the time   ○ Practically all of the time

E. Is the caregiver using positive, reassuring words that help children learn correct labels without criticizing their responses that may not be correct initially?

      ○ Practically never   ○ Most of the time

      ○ Some of the time   ○ Practically all of the time

F. Does the caregiver give children opportunities to express themselves when they work at a creative activity by asking the children about their work?

      ○ Practically never   ○ Most of the time

      ○ Some of the time   ○ Practically all of the time

G. Does the caregiver give children new words when they indicate a readiness to accommodate a new word into their vocabulary?

      ○ Practically never   ○ Most of the time

      ○ Some of the time   ○ Practically all of the time

H. Does the caregiver use open-ended questions with children to encourage thinking and more complex talk?

      ○ Practically never   ○ Most of the time

      ○ Some of the time   ○ Practically all of the time

11. Does the caregiver recognize and take advantage of teachable moments?

When an adult focuses on a situation directly involving the child, this makes it possible to reinforce a desired behavior, to extend understanding of a concept, to help a child make a connection between an emotion and an action, to understand the point of view of another, or to provide a new vocabulary word. Teachers take advantage of teachable moments to enrich the world of children's experience and deepen their knowledge.

A. Does the caregiver notice teachable moments and use them to promote awareness and new understandings?
- ○ Practically never
- ○ Some of the time
- ○ Most of the time
- ○ Practically all of the time

B. Is the caregiver able to put a scheduled curricular plan on hold to concentrate on a meaningful experience that might arise or that a child might introduce?
- ○ Practically never
- ○ Some of the time
- ○ Most of the time
- ○ Practically all of the time

12. Is the caregiver sensitive to the rhythms and pacing of days and activities?

There are varied rhythms to the days children spend in care. Sometimes children are excited, running around shouting outdoors with glee and riding trikes vigorously. Sometimes, all absorbed, they sit in a corner and examine each pinecone or slice of agate on a nature table with a small hand-held magnifying glass. But at the end of some days, some children seem to wilt. They often need a caregiver to caress them and speak in soothing, low, reassuring tones. Younger children may climb up on a teacher's lap and just cuddle quietly.

Transitions can be frustrating for young children. They need lots of notice that an activity is ending. They often need time to wind down. Teachers need to give enough clear notice for a change.

A. Does the caregiver balance opportunities during the day for quiet, more peaceful times and noisy, more boisterous times?
○ Practically never ○ Most of the time
○ Some of the time ○ Practically all of the time

B. Does the caregiver offer opportunities for both small- and large-muscle skill development?
○ Practically never ○ Most of the time
○ Some of the time ○ Practically all of the time

C. Does the caregiver seem sensitive to a child's developmental level and level of tiredness during activities, including meal times when adult requests for neatness might be too hard for a sleepy child to comply with?
○ Practically never ○ Most of the time
○ Some of the time ○ Practically all of the time

D. Does the caregiver give children appropriate notice and encourage peaceful transitions?
○ Practically never ○ Most of the time
○ Some of the time ○ Practically all of the time

13. Does the caregiver promote children's mental health?

Teachers play a valuable role in preventing later mental health problems and promoting positive mental health. They validate children's feelings while teaching the difference between owning one's own feelings and realizing some actions are acceptable and some are not. Children do need adults to acknowledge the reality of their emotions. Children need help in identifying their own and others' emotions accurately. Caregivers who promote good mental health give clear, supportive feedback that a child's feelings and perception of the world are as legitimate as anyone else's. Teachers empower children by offering small choices, carefully considered by the adults as appropriate, whenever possible.

A. Does the caregiver tune in to and sincerely listen to each child's feelings of worry, sadness, or anger, as well as excitement and joy?

- ○ Practically never
- ○ Some of the time
- ○ Most of the time
- ○ Practically all of the time

B. Does the caregiver suggest helpful ideas on how to cope with strong upset or negative feelings?

- ○ Practically never
- ○ Some of the time
- ○ Most of the time
- ○ Practically all of the time

C. Does the caregiver help children to understand their own and other's feelings?

- ○ Practically never
- ○ Some of the time
- ○ Most of the time
- ○ Practically all of the time

D. Does the caregiver encourage autonomy and offer safe choices that allow for individual child preferences when possible?

- ○ Practically never
- ○ Some of the time
- ○ Most of the time
- ○ Practically all of the time

E. Does the caregiver provide positive attributes that affirm the goodness of each child?

- ○ Practically never
- ○ Some of the time
- ○ Most of the time
- ○ Practically all of the time

14. Does the caregiver use a variety of positive discipline techniques for dealing with problem behaviors?

The effective caregiver tries hard to see ahead and prevent problems. Building inner controls among young children takes time, trust, and patience. Having a large supply and variety of positive discipline techniques serves a caregiver well in dealing with puzzling or difficult child behaviors. Creative structuring of learning episodes can minimize child frictions and fusses. Keeping promises consistently is a good technique for building up children's faith that they will get their turn, that there will be enough cookies to go around, and that they will get their needs met. An effective caregiver uses specific praise and encouragement.

A. Does the caregiver use distraction and redirection techniques judiciously?
   - ○ Practically never
   - ○ Some of the time
   - ○ Most of the time
   - ○ Practically all of the time
B. Does the caregiver use dramatic role play to engage a child in more acceptable activities as an alternative to more troublesome ones?
   - ○ Practically never
   - ○ Some of the time
   - ○ Most of the time
   - ○ Practically all of the time
C. Does the caregiver restate clearly and succinctly rules for unacceptable behaviors: "No hitting or hurting," "No throwing toys," "No calling others hurtful names"?
   - ○ Practically never
   - ○ Some of the time
   - ○ Most of the time
   - ○ Practically all of the time
D. Does the caregiver keep promises to a minimum and follow through on promises made?
   - ○ Practically never
   - ○ Some of the time
   - ○ Most of the time
   - ○ Practically all of the time
E. Does the caregiver offer specific praise that encourages desirable behaviors?
   - ○ Practically never
   - ○ Some of the time
   - ○ Most of the time
   - ○ Practically all of the time

15. Does the caregiver instill a love of books, stories, writing, and reading?

Effective teachers admire the slow, steady growth of reading and writing skills. They sing songs, read books, tell stories, share chants, and encourage children's creative writing and reading attempts.

Daily book reading with children is more likely to result in early school success (Jalongo, 2007). Sharing picture books and using dialogic talk about the pictures enhances language skills.

A. Does the caregiver share picture books and read every day with the children?

- ◯ Practically never
- ◯ Some of the time
- ◯ Most of the time
- ◯ Practically all of the time

B. Does the caregiver read with rich emotional tones and sensitivity to children's interests to awaken children's passion for books?

- ◯ Practically never
- ◯ Some of the time
- ◯ Most of the time
- ◯ Practically all of the time

C. Does the caregiver talk about pictures with the children and ask them for their ideas and experiences that might be like those of the storybook characters?

- ◯ Practically never
- ◯ Some of the time
- ◯ Most of the time
- ◯ Practically all of the time

D. Does the caregiver provide work spaces for scribbling and drawing, and opportunities for each child to dictate to the teacher a story that can be acted out in class?

- ◯ Practically never
- ◯ Some of the time
- ◯ Most of the time
- ◯ Practically all of the time

16. Does the caregiver share with the children that she is also an adventurous learner?

Children enjoy learning that their teacher is a learner, too. They get excited when their teacher shares new explorations and adventures with them. To encourage ongoing exploration in early childhood development, directors should provide materials and opportunities for teachers to attend workshops, classes, seminars, or conventions where they can develop their knowledge and grow as caregivers.

A. Does the caregiver share with the children an exciting learning adventure in her own life?

- ◯ Practically never
- ◯ Some of the time
- ◯ Most of the time
- ◯ Practically all of the time

B. Does the caregiver read child-development materials and attend ECE workshops, then arrange to share the excitement of new ideas and learning experiences with the children?

○ Practically never   ○ Most of the time

○ Some of the time   ○ Practically all of the time

17. Can the caregiver put forth the energy required for daily child care work?

Orchestrating daily happenings and working with groups of young children every day, planning for their needs, and individualizing interactions to meet specific needs takes a great deal more energy than many other jobs.

A. Does the caregiver have the physical well-being to care for young children for a full work day?

   ○ Practically never   ○ Most of the time

   ○ Some of the time   ○ Practically all of the time

B. Does the caregiver have the psychological and emotional energy to encourage curiosity and excitement about learning?

   ○ Practically never   ○ Most of the time

   ○ Some of the time   ○ Practically all of the time

18. Does the caregiver provide a positive model for empathy and compassion for the children?

A caregiver who has formed a trusting, loving relationship with a child can teach so much just by the way she behaves. Children learn empathy and caring for others from having consistently experienced nurturing responses. They learn compassion by seeing how adults treat children with compassion. As teachers model enthusiasm for learning, empathy and compassion, kindness and helpfulness, positive discipline methods, and gracious social relations with other staff, children are likely to imitate them.

A. Does the caregiver provide a prosocial role model for empathy, patience, and courtesy with all persons?

   ○ Practically never   ○ Most of the time

   ○ Some of the time   ○ Practically all of the time

B. Does the caregiver notice aloud when children exhibit empathy, kindness, patience, and courtesy?

○ Practically never   ○ Most of the time

○ Some of the time   ○ Practically all of the time

19. Does the caregiver respect the unique temperament style and personhood of each child?

Most children come into the world with one of three major temperament styles: feisty, flexible, or fearful (Honig, 1997b). Feisty children are triggery and intense. A less intense child who has a more flexible temperament adapts more easily to change. Fearful children are apt to act shy and cautious about approaching anything new.

A. Is the caregiver tuned in to each child's temperament style?

○ Practically never   ○ Most of the time

○ Some of the time   ○ Practically all of the time

B. Is the caregiver responsive to any sensory sensitivities a child may have?

○ Practically never   ○ Most of the time

○ Some of the time   ○ Practically all of the time

20. Does the caregiver meet the children's sensuous needs?

Sensory needs are strong. Young children lick and munch on food as if delighted as much with the texture and taste as well as with filling their bellies. When given a hunk of ripe banana, some babies are as likely to find as much pleasure in squishing the banana through fingers as in biting off a bit to munch. While carrying a baby, a caregiver might be amused to see the little one lean down and lick the caregiver's arm. Children are sensuous creatures. Hold a baby up to a mirror and she may lean forward to lick or stroke her own reflection as she vocalizes. A teacher provides "E" vitamins (emotional vitamins) for a tired or worried child by snuggling the child onto a lap for a story or a quiet time or wrapping a comforting arm around the child. Caressing physical gestures also serve as sensuous experiences that nourish the child's positive sense of self while satisfying a child's needs for bodily contact comfort.

A. Does the caregiver peaceably accept the sensuous personal nature of little ones?
- ○ Practically never
- ○ Some of the time
- ○ Most of the time
- ○ Practically all of the time

B. Does the caregiver provide experiences with water play, clay, playdough, fingerpaint, and other sensory experiences?
- ○ Practically never
- ○ Some of the time
- ○ Most of the time
- ○ Practically all of the time

C. Does the caregiver provide sensory experiences by serving foods attractively and by engaging children in sniffing and tasting experiences?
- ○ Practically never
- ○ Some of the time
- ○ Most of the time
- ○ Practically all of the time

D. Does the caregiver plan for and provide outdoor nature experiences for the children?
- ○ Practically never
- ○ Some of the time
- ○ Most of the time
- ○ Practically all of the time

21. Does the caregiver have high, individualized expectations for each child, regardless of ability level?

Children come to the center with different levels of attention span and persistence, as well as varying ability levels. All children need to be challenged in unhurried, unpressured ways to become more competent.

A. Does the caregiver make a concerted effort to learn about each child's strengths and difficulties?
- ○ Practically never
- ○ Some of the time
- ○ Most of the time
- ○ Practically all of the time

B. Does the caregiver support each child's individual level of interest and ability?
- ○ Practically never
- ○ Some of the time
- ○ Most of the time
- ○ Practically all of the time

C. Does the caregiver support acceptance and a nurturing atmosphere in the classroom?
- ⭘ Practically never
- ⭘ Some of the time
- ⭘ Most of the time
- ⭘ Practically all of the time

22. Does the caregiver act to make families feel warmly welcome in the program?

Finding ways to promote good parent-center cooperation for child development is a challenge for the caregiver. Quality caregivers approach family members as a valued source of further information about a child, asking parents to share their special knowledge about their child with staff (Honig, 1975). The caregiver listens to a parent nonjudgmentally, even if the caregiver does not feel that some of the parent's concerns are ones that a teacher can or should deal with. The teacher conveys admiration for the parent who is trying so hard to carry out two important jobs at the workplace and at home. Children watch the ways in which their families and their teachers get along and learn to feel comfortable and secure because they have learned that these relationships are warm and accepting.

A. Does the caregiver find ways to relate with parents so that children notice the teacher's caring and supportive communications with family members at drop-off and pick-up times?
- ⭘ Practically never
- ⭘ Some of the time
- ⭘ Most of the time
- ⭘ Practically all of the time

B. Does the caregiver seem comfortable interacting with children and families who come from different cultural backgrounds and may have limited English-speaking ability?
- ⭘ Practically never
- ⭘ Some of the time
- ⭘ Most of the time
- ⭘ Practically all of the time

C. Does the caregiver offer materials and resources for parents who would like to learn more about child development?
- ⭘ Practically never
- ⭘ Some of the time
- ⭘ Most of the time
- ⭘ Practically all of the time

23. Does the caregiver integrate the day-care experience for children?

Integration should occur along several dimensions: cognitive, language, and problem-solving activities; social and emotional supports; and everyday tasks such as nap times, toileting times, shepherding times, and clean-up times. Ordinary experiences can become enriching intellective experiences that can help children feel not only safe and well cherished but also can provide special learning opportunities. Sensitive planning, awareness, and communication skills are required.

A. Does the caregiver use each daily routine experience as a potential opportunity to address several goals to enrich children's development and maximize early learning?

  ○ Practically never   ○ Most of the time
  ○ Some of the time   ○ Practically all of the time

B. Does the caregiver try the light touch of a bit of simple humor with the children?

  ○ Practically never   ○ Most of the time
  ○ Some of the time   ○ Practically all of the time

24. Is the caregiver a role model for aides, volunteers, less experienced teachers, or student interns?

The last checklist item is exclusively posed as a question that relates to the attributes of seasoned caregivers and teachers who are already professionally highly qualified in their work.

Experienced teachers of young children often help their aides and teachers-in-training develop effective skills through sharing ideas and experiences, providing positive feedback, and modeling successful techniques.

A. Does the seasoned teacher who is designated to help aides, volunteers, and student interns help the newcomers feel welcome by receiving them warmly in the classroom, explaining the daily schedule and classroom routines, and introducing them to co-workers, parents, and children?

○ Practically never   ○ Most of the time

○ Some of the time   ○ Practically all of the time

B. Does the supervising teacher create an environment where those supervised feel comfortable to observe and to participate in planning whenever appropriate?

○ Practically never   ○ Most of the time

○ Some of the time   ○ Practically all of the time

C. Does the supervising teacher provide explanations, comment positively on successful interactions, and ask Socratic questions of those supervised to help them consider and reflect on their efforts?

○ Practically never   ○ Most of the time

○ Some of the time   ○ Practically all of the time

D. Does the experienced teacher take advantage of teachable moments to suggest a variety of activities and interactions that reflect effective techniques and reinforce early childhood principles?

○ Practically never   ○ Most of the time

○ Some of the time   ○ Practically all of the time

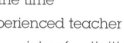

THE ABBREVIATED CARE QUALITY CHECKLIST

The abbreviated checklist makes it possible, after observations have been made over time, for an observer to check a summary rating for each item. Taken together, the profile of checks may portray a caregiver who helps each child flourish intellectually, emotionally, physically, and in developing language power and a passion for learning. Or, the rater's checks on the abbreviated rating sheet may reflect that this caregiver needs more supports to work toward excellence in caregiving. Even when a director has decided to use only some of the categories to observe, this abbreviated form will make it easier to see an overall profile of the items that were the focus of the observations.

When most of the ratings for most of the items are positive, the checklist provides a portrait of a teacher whose caring quotient is very high:

- The teacher supports children as they strive to understand the world they are born into and become autonomous little persons.

- The teacher is capable of making good decisions for her own life.
- The teacher tunes in to children's interests and provides materials, opportunities, and interactions that advance each child's passionate curiosity and desire to learn.
- The teacher affirms each child's conviction that he will grow up to become an effective, and perhaps even unique, player on the stage of life.
- The teacher nourishes in each child the conviction that the child is lovable and competent.
- The teacher supports each child's struggle, even a child with early troubles, to feel confidence in her own worth and capabilities.
- The teacher promotes prosocial behaviors and child friendships.
- The teacher consistently offers children the surety of being understood, listened to, and well-cared for.

Use the ratings gathered over time to give a more positive or less positive score for each item.

1. Is the caregiver a nourisher?
   - ○ Not enough
   - ○ Quite frequently
2. Is the caregiver a good classroom arranger?
   - ○ Not enough
   - ○ Quite frequently
3. Does the room where the children are cared for seem harmonious and aesthetically lovely to live in?
   - ○ Not enough
   - ○ Quite frequently
4. Is the caregiver a good observer?
   - ○ Not enough
   - ○ Quite frequently
5. Does the caregiver encourage competency at everyday personal tasks?
   - ○ Not enough
   - ○ Quite frequently

6. Does the caregiver boost thinking and reasoning skills?
   - O Not enough
   - O Quite frequently

7. Is the caregiver a good "matchmaker"?
   - O Not enough
   - O Quite frequently

8. Does the caregiver encourage creativity and the pleasures of pretend play?
   - O Not enough
   - O Quite frequently

9. Does the caregiver provide positive contingent reinforcement (PCR)?
   - O Not enough
   - O Quite frequently

10. Is the caregiver a language enlarger?
    - O Not enough
    - O Quite frequently

11. Does the caregiver recognize and take advantage of teachable moments?
    - O Not enough
    - O Quite frequently

12. Is the caregiver sensitive to the rhythms and pacing of days and activities?
    - O Not enough
    - O Quite frequently

13. Does the caregiver promote children's mental health?
    - O Not enough
    - O Quite frequently

14. Does the caregiver use a variety of positive discipline techniques for dealing with problem behaviors?
    - O Not enough
    - O Quite frequently

15. Does the caregiver instill a love of books, stories, writing, and reading?
    - O Not enough
    - O Quite frequently

16. Does the caregiver share with the children that she is also an adventurous learner?
    ○ Not enough
    ○ Quite frequently

17. Can the caregiver put forth the energy required for daily child care work?
    ○ Not enough
    ○ Quite frequently

18. Does the caregiver provide a positive model for empathy and compassion for the children?
    ○ Not enough
    ○ Quite frequently

19. Does the caregiver respect the unique temperament style and personhood of each child?
    ○ Not enough
    ○ Quite frequently

20. Does the caregiver meet the children's sensuous needs?
    ○ Not enough
    ○ Quite frequently

21. Does the caregiver have high, individualized expectations for each child, regardless of ability level?
    ○ Not enough
    ○ Quite frequently

22. Does the caregiver act to help families feel warmly welcome at the program?
    ○ Not enough
    ○ Quite frequently

23. Does the caregiver integrate the day-care experience for children?
    ○ Not enough
    ○ Quite frequently

24. Is the caregiver a role model and mentor for aides, volunteers, less-experienced teachers, or student interns?
    ○ Not enough
    ○ Quite frequently

REFERENCES AND RECOMMENDED READINGS

Adcock, Don, and Marilyn Segal. 1983. *Making Friends: Ways of Encouraging Social Development in Young Children.* Englewood Cliffs, NJ: Prentice-Hall.

Ainsworth, Mary. 1979. "Infant-Mother Attachment." *American Psychologist* 34(10): 932–937.

Ainsworth, Mary, and Silvia Bell. 1974. "Mother-Infant Interaction and the Development of Competence." In *The Growth of Competence,* 97–118. New York: Academic Press.

Arnett, Jeffrey. 1989. "Caregivers in Day-Care Centers: Does Training Matter?" *Journal of Applied Developmental Psychology* 10(4): 541–552.

Bandura, Albert, Dorothea Ross, and Sheila Ross. 1963. "Imitation of Film-Mediated Aggressive Models." *Journal of Abnormal and Social Psychology* 66(1): 3–11.

Bayley, Nancy. 2005. *Bayley Scales of Infant and Toddler Development.* 3rd ed. San Antonio, TX: Pearson Assessments.

Blank, Marion. 1975. *Teaching Learning in the Preschool: A Dialogue Approach.* Columbus, OH: Charles E. Merrill.

Bornstein, Marc, Chun-Shin Hahn, Nancy Gist, and Maurice Haynes. 2006. "Long-Term Cumulative Effects of Childcare on Children's Mental Development and Socioemotional Adjustment in a Non-Risk Sample: The Moderating Effects of Gender." *Early Child Development and Care* 176(2): 129–156.

Brophy-Herb, Holly, and Alice Honig. 1999. "Reflectivity: Key Ingredient in Positive Adolescent Parenting." *Journal of Primary Prevention* 19(3): 241–250.

Caldwell, Bettye, and Alice Honig. 1973. "APPROACH: A Procedure for Patterning the Responses of Adults and Children." In *Measures of Maturation: An Anthology of Early Childhood Observation Instruments*, 1: 610–672. Philadelphia, PA: Research for Better Schools.

Cooper, Donna, and Kristina Costa. 2012. *Increasing the Effectiveness and Efficiency of Existing Public Investments in Early Childhood Education: Recommendations to Boost Program Outcomes and Efficiency*. Washington, DC: Center for American Progress.

Copple, Carol, and Sue Bredekamp, eds. 2010. *Developmentally Appropriate Practice in Early Childhood Programs Serving Children from Birth through Age 8*. 3rd ed. Washington, DC: NAEYC.

Copple, Carol, and Sue Bredekamp, eds. 2013. *Developmentally Appropriate Practice: Focus on Infants and Toddlers*. Washington, DC: NAEYC.

Davies, Patrick, Dante Cicchetti, and Meredith Martin. 2012. "Toward Greater Specificity in Identifying Associations among Interparental Aggression, Child Emotional Reactivity to Conflict, and Child Problems." *Child Development* 83(5): 1789–1804.

De-Souza, Desalyn. 2012. "Child Care Center Directors' Perceptions of Continuity of Care: A Qualitative Investigation." PhD diss., Syracuse University.

Eliker, James, Carolyn Langill, Karen Ruprecht, and Kyong-Ah Kwon. 2007. *Paths to QUALITY—A Child Care Quality Rating System for Indiana: What Is Its Scientific Basis?* West Lafayette, IN: Purdue University, Center for Families and Department of Child Development and Family Studies.

Erikson, Erik. 1993. *Childhood and Society*, reissue ed. New York: Norton.

Gardner, Howard. 1993. *Frames of Mind: The Theory of Multiple Intelligences*. New York: Basic.

Gilman, Phoebe. 1992. *Something from Nothing*. New York: Scholastic.

Goleman, Daniel. 1995. *Emotional Intelligence*. New York: Bantam Books.

Gopnik, Alison. 2012. "Why Play Is Serious." *Smithsonian Magazine* July–August: 13.

Greenspan, Stanley, and Serena Wieder. 2005. *Infant and Early Childhood Mental Health: A Comprehensive Developmental Approach to Assessment and Intervention.* Washington, DC: American Psychiatric Association.

Harms, Thelma, Richard Clifford, and Debby Cryer. 2003. *Early Childhood Environment Rating Scale,* rev. ed. New York: Teachers College Press.

Harms, Thelma, Debby Cryer, and Richard Clifford. 2003. *Infant/Toddler Environment Rating Scale,* rev. ed. New York: Teachers College Press.

Hart, Betty, and Todd Risley. 1999. *The Social World of Children Learning to Talk.* Towson, MD: Paul H. Brookes.

Hartup, Willard, and Nan Stevens. 1999. "Friendships and Adaptation across the Life Span." *Current Directions in Psychological Science* 8(3): 76–79.

Honig, Alice. 1975. *Parent Involvement in Early Childhood Education.* Washington, DC: NAEYC.

Honig, Alice. 1982. *Playtime Learning Games for Young Children.* Syracuse, NY: Syracuse University Press.

Honig, Alice. 1993. "Toilet Learning." *Day Care and Early Education* 21(1): 6–9.

Honig, Alice. 1995. "Singing with Infants and Toddlers." *Young Children* 50(5): 72–78.

Honig, Alice. 1996. *Nurturing Young Children's Language Power.* Video. St. Luis Obispo, CA: Davidson Films.

Honig, Alice. 1997a. "Creating Integrated Environments for Young Children." *Early Childhood Education Journal* 25(2): 93–100.

Honig, Alice. 1997b. "Infant Temperament and Personality: What Do We Need to Know?" *Montessori Life* 9(3): 18–21.

Honig, Alice. 2000. "Raising Happy Achieving Children in the New Millennium." *Early Child Development and Care* 163(1): 79–106.

Honig, Alice. 2001a. "Language Flowering, Language Empowering: 20 Ways Parents and Teachers Can Assist Young Children." *Montessori Life* 13(4): 31–35.

Honig, Alice. 2001b. "Promoting Creativity, Giftedness, and Talent in Young Children in Preschool and School Situations." In *Promoting Creativity Across the Life Span*, 83–125. Washington, DC: Child Welfare League of America.

Honig, Alice. 2002a. "Choosing Childcare for Young Children." In *Handbook of Parenting: Practical Issues in Parenting*, 2nd ed., 5: 375–405. Hillsdale, NJ: Lawrence Erlbaum.

Honig, Alice. 2002b. *Secure Relationships: Nurturing Infant/Toddler Attachment in Early Care Settings.* Washington, DC: NAEYC.

Honig, Alice. 2004. "Twenty Ways to Boost Your Baby's Brain Power." *Scholastic Parent and Child* 11(4): 55–56.

Honig, Alice. 2005. *Behavior Guidance for Infants and Toddlers.* Little Rock, AR: Southern Early Childhood Association.

Honig, Alice. 2007. "Play: Ten Power Boosts for Children's Early Learning." *Young Children* 62(5): 72–78.

Honig, Alice. 2008. "Oral Language Development." In *Metacognitive Approaches to Developing Oracy: Developing Speaking and Listening with Young Children*, 13–46. London: Taylor and Francis.

Honig, Alice. 2011. *Little Kids, Big Worries: Stress-Busting Tips for Early Childhood Classrooms.* Baltimore: Paul H. Brookes.

Honig, Alice, and Holly Brophy. 1996. *Talking with Your Baby: Family as the First School.* Syracuse, NY: Syracuse University Press.

Honig, Alice, and Andrea Hirallal. 1998. "What Counts More for Excellence in Childcare Staff: Years in Service, Level of Education, or ECE Coursework?" *Early Child Development and Care* 145(1): 31–46.

Honig, Alice, and Ronald Lally. 1975a. "Assessing Teacher Behaviors with Infants in Day Care." In *Exceptional Infant: Assessment and Intervention*, 3: 528–544. New York: Brunner/Mazel.

Honig, Alice, and Ronald Lally. 1975b. "How Good Is Your Infant Program? Use an Observational Method to Find Out." *Child Care Quarterly* 4(3): 194–207.

Honig, Alice, and Ronald Lally. 1981. *Infant Caregiving: A Design for Training.* 2nd ed. Syracuse, NY: Syracuse University Press.

Honig, Alice, and Patricia Martin. 2009. "Does Brief In-Service Training Help Teachers Increase Their Turn-Taking Talk and Socratic Questions with Low-Income Preschoolers?" *NHSA Dialog: A Research-to-Practice Journal for the Early Childhood Field* 12(1): 33–44.

Honig, Alice, and Arlene Nealis. 2011. "What Do Young Children Dream About?" *Early Child Development and Care* 182(6): 1–25.

Honig, Alice, and Brad Pollack. 1990. "Effects of a Brief Intervention Program to Promote Prosocial Behaviors in Young Children." *Early Education and Development* 1(6): 438–444.

Honig, Alice, and Alyce Thompson. 1994. "Helping Toddlers with Peer Group Entry Skills." *Zero to Three* 14(5): 15–19.

Jalongo, Mary. 2007. *Early Childhood Language Arts.* 4th ed. Boston, MA: Pearson Education.

Kaplan, Louise. 1978. *Oneness and Separateness: From Infant to Individual.* New York: Simon and Schuster.

Katz, Lilian. 2004. *Rearview Mirror: Reflections on a Preschool Car Project.* DVD. Urbana, IL: Early Childhood and Parenting Collaborative, University of Illinois at Champaign Urbana.

Klugman, Edgar, and Sara Smilansky. 1990. *Children's Play and Learning: Perspectives and Policy Implications.* New York: Teachers College Press.

Lally, Ronald, and Alice Honig. 1977. "The Family Development Research Program." In *The Preschool in Action: Exploring Early Childhood Programs,* 2nd ed., 149–194. Boston: Allyn and Bacon.

La Paro, Karen, Amy Thomason, Joanna Lower, Victoria Kintner-Duffy, and Deborah Cassidy. 2012. "Examining the Definition and Measurement of Quality in Early Childhood Education: A Review of Studies Using the ECERS-R from 2003 to 2010." *Early Childhood Research and Practice* 14(1). Urbana, IL: Early Childhood and Parenting Collaborative, University of Illinois at Champaign-Urbana. http://ecrp.uiuc.edu/v14n1/laparo.html.

Lefancheck, Michael. 2012. "System Will Monitor Early Learning Programs." *The Syracuse Post-Standard.* Letter to the editor. June 24. E3.

Lewin-Benham, Ann. 2011. *Twelve Best Practices for Early Childhood Education: Integrating Reggio and Other Inspired Approaches.* New York: Teachers College Press.

Lisonbee, Jared, Jacquelyn Mize, Amie Payne, and Douglas Granger. 2008. "Children's Cortisol and the Quality of Teacher-Child Relationships in Child Care." *Child Development* 79(6): 1818–1832.

Louv, Richard. 2012. "A Call to Nature: We'd All Benefit from More 'Vitamin N.'" *AARP Bulletin.* July/August: 32.

Markman, Ellen, and Jean Hutchinson. 1984. "Children's Sensitivity to Constraints on Word Meaning: Taxonomic versus Thematic Relations." *Cognitive Psychology* 16(1): 1–27.

McClelland, Megan, Claire Cameron, Carol Connor, Carrie Farris, Abigail Jewkes, and Frederick Morrison. 2007. "Links between Behavioral Regulation and Preschoolers' Literacy, Vocabulary, and Math Skills." *Developmental Psychology* 43(4): 947–959.

Morrison, George. 2012. "Racing to the Bottom." *Public School Montessorian* 24(4): 5.

National Association for the Education of Young Children. 2005. *Code of Ethical Conduct and Statement of Commitment.* Position statement. Washington, DC: NAEYC.

National Institute of Child Health and Human Development Early Child Care Research Network. 2002. "Child Care Structure Process Outcome: Direct and Indirect Effects of Child-Care Quality on Young Children's Development." *Psychological Science* 13(3): 199–206.

The Nature Action Collaborative for Children. 2012. "Extend International Mud Day into Everyday Learning." *Wonder* July/August: 97–100.

Neugebauer, Roger. 2012. "Physical and Verbal Imitation." Childcare Exchange.com.

Paley, Vivian. 1986. *Boys and Girls: Superheroes in the Doll Corner.* Chicago, IL: University of Chicago Press.

Piaget, Jean. 1951. *Play, Dreams, and Imitation in Childhood.* Portsmouth, NH: Heinemann.

Piaget, Jean. 1954. *The Construction of Reality in the Child.* New York: Basic Books.

Post-Standard. 2012. "Mental Illness and Young People." June 17, B–7.

Ramey, Craig, and Sharon Ramey. 2007. "Early Learning and School Readiness: Can Early Intervention Make a Difference?" In *Appraising the Human Developmental Sciences: Essays in Honor of Merrill-Palmer Quarterly*. Detroit, MI: Wayne State University Press.

Rigg, Pamela. n.d. *Montessori Rating Scales: Early Childhood-Environment*. http://montessoriratingscales.com.

Roopnarine, Jaipaul. 2013. "Early Child Development, Care, and Education in the Caribbean: The Larger Picture." In *Issues and Perspectives in Early Childhood Development and Education in Caribbean Countries*. San Fernando, Trinidad: Caribbean Educational Publishers.

Sabol, Terri, Sandra Soliday Hong, Robert Pianta, and Margaret Burchinal. 2013. "Can Rating Pre-K Programs Predict Children's Learning?" *Science* 341(6148): 845–846.

Sakellariou, Maria, and Konstantina Rentzou. 2012. "Greek Pre-Service Kindergarten Teachers' Beliefs and Intensions about the Importance of Teacher-Child Interactions." *Early Child Development and Care* 182(1): 123–135.

Saracho, Olivia, and Bernard Spodek, eds. 1998. *Multiple Perspectives on Play in Early Childhood Education*. New York: State University of New York Press.

Schweinhart, Lawrence, H. V. Barnes, and D. P. Weikart. 1993. "Significant Benefits: The HighScope Perry Preschool Study through Age 27." *Monographs of the HighScope Educational Research Foundation, No. 10*. Ypsilanti, MI: HighScope Press.

Setodji, Claude, Vi-Nhuan Le, and Diana Schaack. 2013. "Using Generalized Additive Modeling to Empirically Identify Thresholds within the ITERS in Relation to Toddlers' Cognitive Development." *Developmental Psychology* 49(4): 632–645.

Sharma, Ajay, and Helen Cockerill. 2014. *Mary Sheridan's From Birth to Five Years: Children's Developmental Progress*. 4th edition. Abingdon, UK: Routledge.

Shure, Myrna. 1996. *Raising a Thinking Child: Help Your Young Child to Resolve Everyday Conflicts and Get Along with Others*. New York: Gallery Books.

Siegler, Robert. 2010. "Improving the Numerical Understanding of Children from Low-Income Families." *Child Development Perspectives* 3(2): 118–124.

Sigel, Irving, and Ruth Saunders. 1979. "An Inquiry into Inquiry: Question-Asking as an Instructional Model." In *Current Topics in Early Childhood Education* 11, 169–193.

Smilansky, Sara, and Leah Sheftaya. 1990. *Facilitating Play: A Medium for Promoting Cognitive, Socio-Emotional, and Academic Development in Young Children*. Gaithersburg, MD: Psychosocial and Educational Publications.

Smith, Sheila, William Schneider, and Lee Kreader. 2010. *Features of Professional Development and On-Site Assistance in Child Care Quality Rating Improvement Systems: A Survey of State-Wide Systems*. New York: Columbia University, National Center for Children in Poverty. http://nccp.org/publications/pdf/text_970.pdf.

Sroufe, L. Alan. 1983. "Infant-Caregiver Attachment and Patterns of Adaptation in the Preschool: The Roots of Competence and Maladaptation." In *Minnesota Symposia on Child Psychology* 16: 41–83. Hillsdale, NJ: Erlbaum.

Sroufe, L. Alan. 2005. "Attachment and Development: A Prospective Longitudinal Study from Birth to Adulthood." *Attachment and Human Development* 7(4): 349–367.

Sroufe, L. Alan, and June Fleeson. 1986. "Attachment and the Construction of Relationships." In *Relationships and Development*, 51–71. Hillsdale, NJ: Erlbaum.

Talan, Teri, and Paula Jorde Bloom. 2009. *Business Administration Scale for Family Child Care*. New York: Teachers College Press.

Thomas, Marlo. 2012. "Make Room for Listening: The Role of a Father." *AARP Magazine*. June/July: 69.

Tizard, Barbara, O. Cooperman, A. Joseph, and Jack Tizard. 1972. "Environmental Effects on Language Development: A Study of Young

Children in Long-Stay Residential Nurseries." *Child Development* 43(2): 337–358.

Tough, Joan. 1977. *The Development of Meaning: A Study of Children's Use of Language.* New York: Halstead Press.

Tseng, Vivian. 2012. "Social Policy Report: The Uses of Research in Policy and Practice." *Sharing Child and Youth Development Knowledge,* 26(2). Ann Arbor, MI: Society for Research in Child Development.

Undheim, Anne Mari, and May Britt Drugli. 2012. "Perspective of Parents and Caregivers on the Influence of Full-Time Day-Care Attendance on Young Children." *Early Child Development and Care* 182(2): 233–247.

Vandell, Deborah, and Mary Anne Corasaniti. 1990. "Variations in Early Child Care: Do They Predict Subsequent Social, Emotional, and Cognitive Differences?" *Early Childhood Research Quarterly* 5(4): 555–572.

van den Boom, Dymphna. 1997. "Sensitivity and Attachment: Next Steps for Developmentalists." *Child Development* 68(4): 592–594.

Vermeer, Harriet, and Marinus van IJzendoorn. 2006. "Children's Elevated Cortisol Levels at Daycare: A Review and Meta-Analysis." *Early Childhood Research Quarterly* 21(3): 390–401.

Vygotsky, Lev. 1978. *Mind in Society: The Development of Higher Psychological Processes.* Cambridge, MA: Harvard University Press.

Whitehurst, Grover, David Arnold, Jeffrey Epstein, Andrea Angell, Meagan Smith, and Janet Fischel. 1994. "A Picture Book Reading Intervention in Day Care and Home for Children from Low-Income Families." *Developmental Psychology* 30(5): 679–689.

Wittmer, Donna, and Alice Honig. 1991. "Convergent or Divergent? Teachers' Questions to Three-Year-Old Children in Day Care." *Early Child Development and Care* 68(1): 141–147.

Wolf, Dennie, ed. 1986. *Connecting: Friendship in the Lives of Young Children and Their Teachers.* Redmond, WA: Exchange Press.

Zelazo, Philip, and Kristen Lyons. 2012. "The Potential Benefits of Mindfulness Training in Early Childhood: A Developmental Social Cognitive Neuroscience Perspective." *Child Development Perspectives* 6(2): 154–160.

Zellman, Gail, Richard Brandon, Kimberly Boller, and Lee Kreader. 2011. *Effective Evaluation of Quality Rating and Improvement Systems for Early Care and Education and School-Age Care*. Washington, DC: Office of Planning, Research and Evaluation, Administration for Children and Families, U.S. Department of Health and Human Services. http://www.acf.hhs.gov/sites/default/files/opre/quality_rating.pdf.

Zigler, Edward, and E. Freedman. 1990. "Psychological Developmental Implications of Current Patterns of Early Child Care." In *Psychosocial Issues in Day Care*, 3–20. Washington, DC: American Psychiatric Press.

INDEX

Multiple intelligences, 31–32
Muscle control, 28–29
Musical experiences, 70, 113, 137
Mutuality, 46

N
Numerical understanding, 13

O
Observation, 55–57, 108, 120–121, 134–135, 152
Open-ended materials, 52–53, 133
Open-ended questions, 12, 77, 139

P
Pacing, 81–83, 140–141, 153
Parallel play, 67
Parallel talk, 75
Parent meetings, 128–129
Parentese, 26
Patience, 15, 25, 34, 103
Peer interactions, 12, 29, 53, 68–69
Persistence, 108–109
Personal interactions, 45–117
    acting as a role model, 116–117
    acting as a matchmaker, 62–63, 74
    arranging the classroom, 51–55
    boosting thinking skills, 59–62
    encouraging competency, 57–59
    encouraging creativity, 63–70
    encouraging language development, 72–78
    encouraging literacy, 97–99
    holding high expectations, 108–109
    integrating experiences, 114–116
    maintaining energy, 100–101
    meeting children's needs, 105–107
    modeling empathy, 101–103
    nourishing children, 46–51
    observing children, 55–57
    promoting mental health, 83–92
    providing positive reinforcement, 71, 74

respecting children, 104
sensitivity to environment, 81–83
sharing love of learning, 99–100
teachable moments, 78–81
using positive discipline, 93–96
welcoming families, 109–114
Personal reflectivity, 13
Play, 12, 16–17, 24, 52–53, 56–57, 63–70, 96, 137–138, 153
Positive contingent reinforcement, 71, 74, 138, 153
Positive discipline techniques, 93–96, 142–143, 153
Powerlessness, 90
Prematurity, 29
Problem behaviors, 71, 86
Problem-solving activities, 117
Project Approach, 52
Projects, 12, 52

Q
Quality care
    defining, 12–15
    developmental milestones, 19–32
    ingredients of, 19–43
    social-emotional learning, 32–43
Quality rating and improvement systems, 13–14

R
Reading skills, 12, 64–65, 97–99, 143–144
Reasoning skills, 20, 59–62, 69, 77, 136
Receptive language, 27
Redirecting, 93, 143
Reflective listening, 87
Reflective supervision, 46
Respect, 104, 146
Rhyming skills, 64, 97
Rhythm, 70, 81–83, 137, 140–141
Role models, 116–117
Role play, 96, 138, 143
Rules, 86, 110, 143

S

Science skills, 61–62

Secure attachment bonding, 37–43, 49

Self-confidence, 57–59

Self-control, 11, 13, 32

Self-stimulation, 106–107

Self-talk, 75

Sensory needs, 105–107, 116, 146–147, 154

Sensory processing troubles, 35–36

Separation anxiety, 37–43, 46–48

Separation-individuation process, 83–84

Sequencing skills, 77

Shyness, 34, 68–69, 104, 121, 146

Size, 60

Social-emotional learning, 9, 20, 24–25, 32–43, 56–57, 68–69, 71, 83–92, 115

Sorting skills, 59–60

Spatial skills, 20

Special needs, 29–30, 120–121

Specific praise, 94–96, 143

Staff turnover, 14–15, 46

Stranger anxiety, 36–37, 48

Stress, 47

Student interns, 116–117, 123–124, 149–150

Superior pincer prehension, 21–22

T

Teachable moments, 78–81, 140, 153

Teacher training, 8–9, 12, 21, 99–100, 144–145

benefits of, 11

Teacher's aides, 116–117, 149–150

Teacher-child interactions, 8–9, 15–17, 34

Teacher-child ratios. See Child-teacher ratios

Temperament types, 33–35, 104, 106, 146, 154

Toilet training, 24, 29

Transitions, 43, 82, 92, 140–141

Trust, 15–17, 49–50

V

Validating kindness, 90

W

Walking, 22

Websites

American Speech-Language-Hearing Association, 27

First Years, 20

PBS, 20

Windows of development, 21–25

Wrist control, 22, 31, 61, 116

Writing skills, 97–99, 143–144

Z

Zone of proximal development, 32, 63